The Golden Retriever

Its Care and Training

Joan Tudor

Series Editor
Dennis Kelsey-Wood

Books Ltd, Edlington,
Horncastle, Lincs, England

First published 1979
by K & R Books Ltd,
Edlington, Lincolnshire

ISBN 0 903264 33 1
Cover Photograph:
Ch. Camrose Fabius Tarquin. Photo: Diane Pearce

Typeset by Woolaston Parker Ltd., and printed by Litho Letter-press Service, both of Leicester, England, and bound in Great Britain by Hunter & Foulis Ltd., of Edinburgh

Contents

List of Illustrations   4

Authors Acknowledgements and Introduction   6

Goldens in Various Roles in Life   7

The History of the Breed   13

Choosing your Puppy   23

Puppy Rearing and Early Training   30

General Care of the Adult Golden   39

The Kennel Club Breed Standard and its Interpretation   45

Breeding   58

Care of the Bitch and Puppies to eight Weeks   74

Showing your Golden Retriever   82

Training to the Gun and Field Trials   92

Appendix
    1 Bibliography   101
    2 Specialist Breed Clubs   102

Index   103

List of Illustrations

Colour
A lovely study of Goldens and friends by Diane Pearce
                                              Front endpapers
Goldens are always ready to play   8
Sh. Ch. Rossbourne Timothy   11
Australian Ch. Queenee Debonair CDX QC   14
A relaxed study of Ch. Camrose Nicolas of Westley   18
A head study to show how, with growing age, the face
   goes partly grey   20
A young puppy   24
A good show prospect at 8 weeks old   27
Ch. Pippa of Westley   32
Six appealing puppies of 8 weeks old   36
Sh. Ch. Camrose Matilda at 8½ years old   41
Goldens mix well with all other breeds   43
A Golden poses with his friend, a Black and Tan Terrier   46
The darkest colour permissible by the standard   52
Two differing heads and coat colour variations   59
Ch. Camrose Fabius Tarquin   63
The two extremes of colour permitted by the standard   69
Goldens have a penchant for digging and getting dirty   72
Typical kind, alert head study   76
Another typical head study but of different "type"   77
Ch. Camrose Nicolas of Westley   81
Good friends!   84
Am. Ch. Beaumaris Dalesman CD   87
"Setting up" a puppy to assess its show potential   90
The best way for a Golden to travel   94
An excellent group study   99
Ch. Styal Stefanie of Camrose (whelped 1973).
   Photo: Diane Pearce   *Rear endpapers*

Black and White
Am. Ch. Footprint of Yeo CD, an outstanding sire with
   12 Champions to his credit. Owned by Carol T. Vogel *Frontispiece*
Ch. Davern Figaro   9
Int. Ch. Cindy Fan It Fokheehoal   10
Australian Ch. Buffalo Woodbuff   12

Ch. Colin of Rosecott   15
Ch. Michael of Moreton   17
A pre-war winner Ch. Davie of Yelme   19
A pre-war bitch Ch. Torrdale Betty   21
Goldens enjoying a romp in the water   25
Who could resist this group of youngsters?   26
An early show winner   28
A Golden Retriever puppy at 3½ months old   31
A fine study of a Golden   34
Camrose Lucine at one year old   35
A one-year-old Golden Retriever   37
Sh. Ch. Gyrima Ariadne   40
Sh. Ch. Stenbury Seasonnet in show stance   42
Ch. Stolford Happy Lad   48
Int. Ch. Camrose Evenpatrol CD, TD (Berm.)   56
Sh. Ch. Grima Pipparetta   60
Sh. Ch. Nortonwood Faunus   62
A very light-coloured Golden   66
Treunair Treubach returning to owner over water   68
Dutch Dual Ch. Andy van Sparrenrode   73
Ch. Brambletyne Carrock Fell of Daryock   75
Am. and Eng. Ch. Figaro of Yeo   79
Ch. Camrose Cabus Christopher, the breed's all-time
   top winner   83
Dual Ch. Andy van Sparrenrode and Golden Chap Beijeren   85
Irish and Eng. Ch. Bryanstown Gale Warning   88
Miss Lumsden handling in a Field Trial   93
Ch. Synspur Lunic   95
A Golden seen retrieving teal   96, 97
Ch. Teecon Ambassador   100

Line Drawings
Glossary of terms   44
Correct and faulty heads   47
Correct and faulty shoulder blade placement   50
Correct and faulty forelegs   51
Correct and faulty pasterns   51
Correct and faulty hindlegs   53
Correct and faulty tail sets   55
Correct and faulty stifles   55
Correct and faulty feet   55
Gestation table   64
A typical whelping box   67
Puppy presenting in normal manner   71
Hind presentation of a puppy   71

Acknowledgements

I must acknowledge the help which I had in the production of the line-drawings for this book. These were very kindly compiled by my partner in the "Camrose" Goldens, Miss Rosemary Wilcock. I am no artist, and without her participation, the finished product would not have been recognisable! I must also thank my long-suffering husband, for his help in taking over so many of the daily kennel chores, whilst I have been occupied in writing this book.

Introduction

Having been a breeder of these lovely dogs for more years than I care to remember, I can assure the aspiring owner, that if this is the breed they decide on, they can be prepared to have many happy years ahead of them.

The Golden Retriever, to be typical of its breed, must have a kindly yet intelligent nature, must be tolerant and loving towards all ages of children and adults, must not be quarrelsome with other dogs, and must look like the breed it represents, and be capable of doing the work for which it was bred.

In this book, I have written chapters on all aspects of the Golden Retriever, and sincerely hope these will be of some help to both novice and experienced owners alike.

Joan Tudor
Burstow
Surrey
1978

Chapter 1

Goldens in Various Roles in Life

Having owned, and been owned by, many Golden Retrievers for over 30 years, I think I can write with some authority on the important part they play in one's life and affections. They are such well-adjusted, responsive dogs, and they adapt well to various types of life, in fact, are a multi-purpose dog.

The Family Pet
The part Goldens play in one's life, as a family dog, is of the utmost importance to both animal and human. For me, the home would not be complete without several Golden Retrievers occupying it. They are so easy to train to the life you require them to have, and are unobtrusive in the house. Clean in their habits, amenable to discipline and fun-loving, their main object in life is to please their owners.

Goldens are very gentle with children and seem to establish a natural rapport with them. They love to join in with children's games, and do not appear to resent the somewhat rough treatment meted out to them from time to time by the youngest members of the family. It must be stressed however that the dog should be allowed complete freedom from disturbance when sleeping, particularly when in its own bed, and parents should discourage the youngsters from pestering the dog too much.

Goldens are the ideal huse-dogs, for they have a great sense of property. They will give warning at the approach of anyone, by barking, and the noise they make is sufficient to warn off any undesirable person. This trait in their character, makes them even more valuable as family pets, for they will warn without attacking. Immediately a stranger is admitted into your midst, he or she is regarded as a friend and accepted as part of the family, but you do know that if the dog is left on his own in the house, he will protect your home from intruders with the gruff, off-putting bark of a big dog.

When this breed is required as a family pet, they must have

Goldens are always ready to play—in this case with a very young German Shepherd puppy. Photo: Diane Pearce

Ch. Davern Figaro. Photo: C. M. Cooke

their own toys, for they love to have their "presents" to carry around and show to each visitor to the house. Their natural instinct, as a gundog born and bred, should be encouraged, and this is to carry. However, it is very annoying when one's best shoes, gloves or handbag, are the objects of their retrieving practice. Endearing as the carrying characteristic is, it is not amusing when one's lounge cushions become the "present", as happened regularly with one of my dogs – when not carrying the cushion, he used it as a head-rest when lying down! For this reason it is essential to provide him with his own toys.

Out of doors, a Golden's greatest pleasure is to retrieve to you, and much exercise can be given to the dog, and your own legs saved, by throwing something for him to bring back to you – his own toy, a stuffed sock, or a ball are equally acceptable to him.

The Working Gundog

Primarily, the Golden Retriever as a breed, was evolved as a gundog, and used for hunting for, and retrieving of, dead or wounded game. This is the sphere in which he excels, and in which he enjoys the use of all his inherited characteristics – an

The only Int. Ch. Golden in Holland—Cindy Fan It Fokheehoal

excellent nose, hunting and retrieving ability. All of us who train and work our dogs with the gun, know the great excitement which they show as soon as the "shooting gear" appears! It is almost as though they say "this is the life for us"!

Goldens are so easy to train to the gun, and make excellent dogs for the rough shooter, the wildfowler, or for the man who is fortunate enough to take part in more formal shoots. They can be trained to hunt for live game as well as being used as a non-slip retriever (this is one which sits beside its owner during shooting, and only retrieves on command). The Golden can reach great heights of perfection in his work, providing his owner has the patience, and the know-how, to guide him along the right lines.

Guide Dogs for the Blind
Goldens, with their steady, amenable temperament, have proved their worth as Guide Dogs for the Blind. Many are trained at the various Centres in England, and there are also breeding establishments in which Goldens are reared from baby puppies, "temperament tested", and if proving suitable, are put in homes with "puppy walkers". These temporary owners offer a home-life for the puppy, with basic training, until it is old enough to go back to the Centre for proper training as a Guide Dog.

It is a proud day, if one has donated a puppy to this cause, when the letter and photo comes of the Golden which has "passed out" as a fully fledged Guide Dog, and is with its new blind owner.

Mountain Rescue Dogs

Goldens have, over the last few years, proved themselves as excellent mountain rescue dogs, being able to find people buried many feet under the snow, and in Scotland, several have taken a training course for this work, and passed out with flying colours. In Norway this is a regular training for Goldens, for many go with their owners when ski-ing, and this could prove most useful in adverse weather conditions.

Show Dogs

The beauty of this breed leads many people who buy a Golden as a pet, to enter it into the showring. Showing your Golden can become a very absorbing hobby, especially if the dog is lucky enough to come home with a prize card or rosette, and many now well-established show kennels have started from such modest beginnings.

Sh. Ch. Rossbourne Timothy, owned by Mrs. J. Burnett

In order to enter a dog at a show, he must first be registered at the Kennel Club in the Active Register, in his owner's name. Advertisements of shows appear in both *Dog World* and *Our Dogs*, about six weeks or so before the show is to be held, and an entry usually has to be made up to four weeks before the show date, on a special form obtainable from the Show Secretary.

If you aspire to show the dog, it is essential to have some idea of procedure, and to find out what is required of both yourself and the dog beforehand. Visit several shows before you enter the dog, and talk to exhibitors to find out how to trim, stand and move the dog. Various Dog Show Societies all over the country run ringcraft classes, at which you will be taught how to show the dog to the best advantage. These classes help the dog as well as the owner, to assimilate the atmosphere of a show, get it used to being handled by strangers, and to meeting strange dogs of various breeds.

Australian Ch. Buffalo Woodbuff, owned by S. Sullivan and S. Henry

Chapter 2

The History of the Breed

Origins
The Golden Retriever as a breed has been in being for just over a
century, though liver or yellow retrievers were occasionally
known much earlier than this, and they occurred in the litters of
black Retrievers.

A yellow pup from such a black Retriever litter became the
forebear of all our present-day Golden Retrievers. He was a dog
called Nous and was obtained by the first Lord Tweedmouth in
about 1864, when he was visiting Brighton. This dog is listed in
the kennel records of Lord Tweedmouth as being "Lord
Chichester's breed". Whelped June, 1864, he is believed to have
come from a litter of all black puppies, though he himself was
yellow.

Nous, according to Lord Tweedmouth's records was later
mated to a liver-coloured Tweed Water Spaniel (a breed of mostly
liver-coloured dogs used on the banks of the Tweed, and looking
somewhat retrieverish in type) called Belle. This pairing produced
four yellow puppies and from these are descended our Goldens as
a breed today.

Lord Tweedmouth's home was at Guisachan in Scotland, and
he kept some of the dogs he bred for himself, others went to local
game-keepers and others to friends and relatives. He met-
iculously kept kennel records of all matings, and through these
records, now kept for posterity in the Kennel Club's library, we are
able to trace down some of the lines to the present-day.

In 1960 the Kennel Club officially recognised this origin of the
breed as correct, and now publishes the following in their Crufts'
Catalogues:

The origin of the Golden Retriever is less obscure than most of the
Retriever varieties, as the breed was definitely started by the first Lord
Tweedmouth last century, as shown in his carefully kept private stud book
and notes, first brought to light by his great-nephew, the Earl of Ilchester,

Australian Ch. Queenee Debonair C.D.X. Q.C., owned by Mrs. N. Bolton and Mr. R. D. Richardson

in 1952. In 1868 Lord Tweedmouth mated a yellow Wavy-coated Retriever [Nous] he had bought from a cobbler in Brighton (bred by Lord Chichester) to a Tweed Water-Spaniel [Belle] from Ladykirk on the Tweed. These Tweed Water-Spaniels, rare except in the Border Country, are described by authorities of the time as like a small Retriever, liver-coloured and curly-coated. Lord Tweedmouth methodically line-bred down from his mating between 1868 and 1890, using another Tweed Water-Spaniel, and outcrosses of two black Retrievers, an Irish Setter and a sandy coloured Bloodhound. (It is now known that one of the most influential kennels in the first part of this century which lies behind all present day Golden Retrievers was founded on stock bred by Lord Tweedmouth)...

We are greatly indebted to Mrs. Elma Stonex for bringing to light a lot of the facts, and for delving into the past history so deeply. She spent 10 years trying to piece facts together, by contacting the family of the first Lord Tweedmouth, and other people who were involved with him. The details and results of Mrs. Stonex's research, and the various pedigrees she worked out to link the past to the present, are gone into in much greater detail than is possible here, in my book *The Golden Retriever*, published by Popular Dogs, Ltd.

Before the true origin of the breed was determined, it was believed that they came from a troupe of Russian Circus dogs purchased by Lord Tweedmouth, and this was believed by all the earlier breeders, and is the story told in Mrs. W. M. Charlesworth's book on the breed, unfortunately now out of print.

There have certainly been dogs with some similarity of type to the old yellow retriever known in Russia for over a century, and they are reported as being used as sheepdogs in the Caucasus, and as gundogs in Siberia. However, there does not appear to be any reason to connect these in any way with the Golden Retriever as we know it today.

The Breed up to 1920

It was only in 1913 that Golden Retrievers were given a separate register in the Kennel Club, and until then they had been registered as Flat- or Wavy-coated Retrievers. They then became known as Retrievers (Golden or Yellow) and in 1920 they became Retrievers (Golden).

The first great pioneer of the breed was Mrs. W. M. Charlesworth whose prefix was "Noranby", and her great

Ch. Colin of Rosecott, an early breed winner. Photo: F. W. Simms

enthusiasm for the breed continued until her death after the second World War. She did much to put Goldens in the public eye, fearlessly showing her dogs all over the country, and by competing extensively in Field Trials. She made up the first-ever Champion in the breed, Ch. Noranby Campfire, and later had many others, all of which were true dual-purpose dogs, with Field Trial awards to their credit. The culminating point in her career must have been when she made up a Dual Champion after the second World War – this was Dual Champion Noranby Destiny. Mrs. Charlesworth founded the Golden Retriever Club in 1920, and the Standard of the breed was then drawn up, and this has hardly changed until the present time, having only been amended in one or two small points.

Other pioneers of the breed were Lord Culham, whose Culham Copper and Culham Brass are well-known names in breed history; the Hon. Mrs. Grigg, whose Kentford Champions were amongst some of the earliest, and Mr. Herman, whose prefix was "Balcombe", and made famous by Dual Ch. Balcombe Boy. Another enthusiast of about the same period was Col. le Poer Trench, who started a separate register of dogs called Retrievers (Russian Yellow), and he bred these under the "St. Huberts" prefix, but no more were recorded at the Kennel Club after 1917.

Another kennel of note during this period was that of Mr. D. Macdonald with his "Ingestre's", these were directly descended from the original Guisachan dogs, and some of the matings he did have played a great part in the establishing of the breed. Mr. J. Eccles (Haulstone) was another breeder of that era who produced several Champions and Field Trial Champions, and Lieut. Col. the Hon. D. Carnegie (Heydown) was another who had a kennel which is noteworthy, for he had Champions and Field Trial winners. The last kennel of note during that period which I will mention here was that of Mr. H. Jenner, who produced many Champions for his "Abbots" prefix, but, although founded during that time most of his winners were to come later.

The Breed Between the Wars

As time went on and the Golden Retriever became more widely known, its popularity spread, and more and more people joined the growing list of owners and breeders.

Again I must say how indebted we are to Mrs. Stonex for her extensive work on pedigrees, and her efforts have led her to the conclusion that most of our Goldens trace their origins to one or more of four matings which took place between 1920 – 25. These were the matings of Glory of Fyning to Stagden Cross Pamela, Dual

Ch. Michael of Moreton, a well known pre-war winner. Photo: Thomas Fall

Ch. Balcombe Boy to Balcombe Bunty, Binks of Kentford to Balvaig and Rory of Bently to Aurora.

Some of the greatest sires of the years between the wars trace their ancestry to these matings. Gilder, the greatest sire of them all having produced 8 Champions, goes back to two of these matings, Ch. Michael of Moreton (sire of 7 Champions and a Show Champion); Ch. Heydown Grip (also sire of 7 Champions); Ch. Cubbington Diver (sire of 5 Champions), and Ch. Diver of Woolley and Ch. Cornelius, both of whom sired several Champions, all trace their ancestry to some of these matings.

Many breeders enjoyed considerable success during this period but Mr. Jenner probably had more success than anyone else, for he produced 15 title-holders. His prefix of "Abbots" will never be forgotten, and he had the honour of producing one of the most influential dogs of the period. This was one that he bred, but who won in the name of Mr. R. L. Kirk, and was called Ch. Michael of Moreton (winner of 17 c.c.'s and sire of 7 Champions). Another great dog, Ch. Davie of Yelme (winner of 10 c.c.'s) also originated here, though his successes were whilst he was in Mr. Wentworth Smith's great "Yelme" kennel.

Mrs. Cottingham's "Woolley" kennel was responsible for the making of 10 Champions and Show Champions, starting in the

1920's. During this period Mrs. Charlesworth continued with her successes in both the showring and at trials, and she made up a total of 8 Champions. Others responsible for a number of titleholders during this era were Lieut. Col. the Hon. D. Carnegie (Heydown), Mr. and Mrs. Eccles' "Haulstone", Mr. and Mrs. Venables Kirk and their "Anningsley", including Dual Ch. Anningsley Stingo, and Mrs. I. Parsons (Torrdale).

Mrs. Nairn's "Stubbings" kennel was probably the largest of the time and she had many good winners and Field Trial award winners. This kennel was carried on in the Post-War period by her daughter, Miss S. Nairn who later, as Mrs. S. Winston, became President of the Golden Retriever Club.

Many of the kennels mentioned above were dual purpose ones, and their owners competed successfully in trials, so they were able to keep the working instincts of the breed, as well as breeding to the Standard.

A delightfully relaxed study of Ch. Camrose Nicolas of Westley. Photo: Sally Anne Thompson

A pre-war winner, Ch. Davie of Yelme. Photo: Thomas Fall

The Breed Post-war

The war years meant the suspension of shows and trials and breeding came practically to a stand-still though many people kept a nucleus of dogs with which to start again after the war. These were not necessarily all of the highest quality, and the immediate post-war years saw a very great divergence in type, and it was only through the efforts of conscientious breeders that the overall type and quality improved, so that by the 1960's the breed was in a very strong position, and has continued so ever since.

Gradually, as the Golden's wonderful nature and good looks became appreciated, the breed gained in popularity, until today it has very high registrations, and at shows usually has one of the highest entries of all breeds.

Top-Winning Show Dogs of the Period

Since the war the breed has brought forth well over 150 Champions and over 100 Show Champions.

Of the really great dogs and bitches those who must be mentioned first are those which have achieved the title of Dual Champion. There have only been three such since the war and these were Mrs. Charlesworth's owner-bred bitch Dual Ch.

19

A head study to show how, with growing age, the face goes partly grey.
Photo: Sally Anne Thompson

Noranby Destiny, Mr. Hickmott's Dual Ch. Stubblesdown Golden Lass (bred by Mr. Jessamy) and English and Irish Dual Ch. David of Westley owned by Miss L. Ross, but bred by Miss J. Gill. Dual Ch. Stubblesdown Golden Lass has had a great part to play in the development of the Field Trial dogs of the 1960's and 70's, as her bloodlines are carried by many of today's trial winners.

The 1950's produced three outstanding show dogs, who dominated the ring for several years, dividing most of the available c.c.'s between them. These were Mrs. L. Pilkington's Ch. Alresford Advertiser – who won 35 c.c.'s, Mrs. Harrison's Ch. Boltby Skylon (29 c.c.'s) who also became a notable sire, and Miss J. Gill's Ch. Simon of Westley with 21 c.c.'s. The first and the last were both winners at trials, so were truly dual-purpose dogs.

The top c.c. winners of the 1960's were Miss Gill's Ch. Camrose Nicolas of Westley (20 c.c.'s and Field Trial awards) and Ch. Camrose Tallyrand of Anbria (16 c.c.'s) who sired 7 full Champions.

The 1970's brought forth the top c.c. winning dog of all times in Ch. Camrose Cabus Christopher. This dog won 41 c.c.'s, all under different judges, and also won 8 Gundog Groups, 2 Best in Shows and 3 Res. Best in Shows, all at All-Breed Championship shows. He was bred in the "Cabus" kennel by Mrs. Moriarty. Christopher ties with the pre-war Gilder as the record-holder as a Champion producer (8). However, he far exceeds all other dogs with his total number of title-holders, for this is 15 to date. His closest rival during his show career was Mrs. P. Robertson's Ch. Stolford Happy Lad, who has won 19 c.c.'s at the time of writing.

The top c.c. winning bitches of the post-war period were Miss Gill's Ch. Pippa of Westley (17 c.c.'s) and she was also a Field Trial award winner, Mrs. Harrison's Sh. Ch. Janville Renown and Mr. J. Raymond's Sh. Ch. Gainspa Florette of Shiremoor who both won 14 c.c.'s, and Mrs. Sawtell's Ch. Deerflite Endeavour of Yeo who won 12 c.c.'s.

Field Trial Dogs

There have been between 30 and 40 Field Trial Champions made up since the war, and many of these have originated from Mrs. Atkinson's "Holway" kennel, or are descended from her dogs.

The two Field Trial Champions whose names must always be thought of before others are those which have won the Retriever Championship, namely Mrs. Lumsden's F.T.Ch. Treunair Cala and Mrs. Atkinson's F.T.Ch. Mazurka of Wynford. Mrs. Atkinson also won second place in the Championship with F.T.Ch. Holway Zest. Two other Field Trial Champions to distinguish themselves by outstanding wins are Mr. Baldwin's F.T.Ch. Holway Teal of

A pre-war bitch, Ch. Torrdale Betty. Photo: Thomas Fall

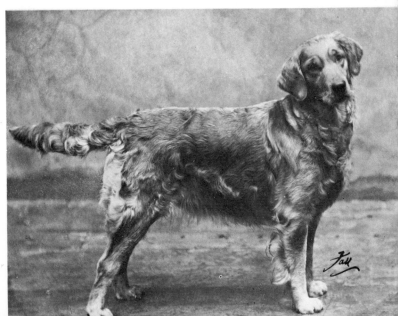

Westley, bred by Miss Gill, and Mrs. Atkinson's F.T.Ch. Holway Gaiety, who both won their F.T.Ch. titles twice over.

Outstanding Sires

Most of the kennels which have produced consistently good trial or show dogs over the years owe their successes in part to Mrs. Stonex's Dorcas Bruin (a res.c.c. winner), for many top Goldens are descended from him through two of his sons, Ch. Dorcas Glorious of Slat and Dorcas Timberscombe Topper. These include the field trial dogs produced in the early 1950's from the mating of Ch. Dorcas Glorious of Slat to Dual Ch. Stubblesdown Golden Lass, and those produced in the showring from the mating of Dorcas Timberscombe Topper and Golden Camrose Tess. Other kennels also owe their success partially to Mrs. Stonex's line through Dorcas Leola, and through Mrs. Harrison's Boltby line.

The leading sires of the 1950's were Ch. Boltby Skylon and Ch. Camrose Fantango, whilst the 1960's brought forth Ch. Camrose Tallyrand of Anbria, Ch. Camrose Nicolas of Westley, Int. Ch. Cabus Cadet, Int. Ch. Cabus Boltby Combine and Ringmaster of Yeo. All these dogs were responsible for siring many title-holders. Undisputed in the 1970's as the top sire in the breed has been Ch. Camrose Cabus Christopher, for he won the Stud Dog Cup for 6 years with record numbers of points, and his progeny won a record number of c.c.'s.

In the field trial world the dog to produce more Field Trial Champions than any other is Mrs. Atkinson's F.T.Ch. Westhyde Holway Zeus, but many of today's field trial winners are the progeny of her F.T.Ch. Holway Zest and Mr. Baldwin's F.T.Ch. Palgrave Holway Folly.

Influential Kennels

There are very few kennels which have been in existence since the 1950's and are still having an influence on the breed, but those which have consistently produced title-holders during the post-war period are Mr. Baldwin (Palgrave), Mrs. Barron (Anbria), Mrs. Borrow (Deerflite), Mrs. Fraser (Westhyde), Miss Gill (Westley – now in partnership with Mrs. Philpott), Wing. Com. and Mrs. Iles (Glennessa), Mrs. Medhurst (Kuldana), Mrs. Minter (Stenbury), Mrs. Moriarty (Cabus), Mrs. Robertson (Stolford), Mrs. Sawtell (Yeo), Mr. Tripptree (Brambletyne), Mrs. Tudor (Camrose – now in partnership with Miss Wilcock).

Others to start later and to have their strains widely spread throughout the country and to have produced several title-holders are Mrs. Birkin (Sansue), Mr. and Mrs. Lowe (Davern), Mrs. Timson (Gyrima) and Mr. and Mrs. Tiranti (Teecon).

Chapter 3

Choosing your Puppy

Is a Golden Retriever the Dog for you?

Before finally deciding that a Golden Retriever is the breed of dog you want, you must take into consideration many factors. For instance, is there someone in the family at home for most of the day? This is essential for all dogs, and especially Goldens, who need human companionship for most of their lives. A dog which is left alone for hours becomes bored, and a bored dog is an anti-social one. He may soon start to chew the furniture, scrape the paint off the doors, pull the wallpaper off the walls, and tear at the carpets. This is not because he is a bad dog, but because he has bad owners.

Next, is someone prepared to devote time to exercising him well each day? All house pets need the experience of sharing walks with their owners, and Goldens which are not exercised properly soon become fat and lazy. The excitement of going for a walk is one of the high-lights in a Golden's day, and he soon learns to recognise the rattle of his leash being taken from its hook, and will be at your feet, dancing with excitement!

Another important factor to consider before purchasing a Golden is the cost of the food required to keep him healthy and happy. It is not possible to give even an approximate cost of feeding an adult Golden, as food prices vary so much from place to place, but it can soon be assessed on current prices when you note his minimum daily requirements. These are about 1 lb meat and 12 oz – 1 lb of biscuit meal.

You must also consider whether or not your home is the correct environment for one of this breed. A flat certainly is not a suitable home for one, unless it is downstairs, and has a garden, and neither is a house which has no suitable free exercising ground near. All dogs need a good free run daily, as well as road walking, in order to keep their muscles in trim.

Lastly, but also of great importance, is to discover if all the family want a Golden Retriever. The home is not a happy one for the dog if he is not welcomed by all its members, particularly the lady of the household. She it is who, most likely, has the responsibility of looking after him. She it is who usually feeds him, and has him around her feet all day long. She is the person who has to wipe up his muddy paw marks, and Hoover up all his hairs from the carpets – and remember, Goldens do have very heavy moults periodically.

Deciding Where to Buy your Puppy

For whatever reason you require your Golden, it is advisable to ensure the kennel you buy it from is one which has its dogs tested for Hereditary Defects. There are hereditary eye defects to which this breed is subject, as well as the usual one of Hip Displasia, common to many other breeds.

It is essential to decide, before buying your puppy, that he will grow up to be the type of Golden you most admire, and with the characteristics you require. Within the breed there is a great variation of type, according to the bloodlines from which the dog comes. Some kennels breed their Goldens specifically as show

A young puppy just itching to get out and about. Photo: Diane Pearce

Goldens enjoying a romp in the water. Photo: Diane Pearce

dogs whilst others breed with only the shooting field in mind. There are others who take care to breed with the standard in mind, and also endeavour to keep the Golden's natural instincts to the fore, so that they are capable of being trained to both show and gun.

It is advisable to buy your puppy from a reputable, private breeder, rather than go to a large kennel which sells puppies of various breeds, which have possibly been bought by them at a very tender age, thus causing the puppies to be inferior and ill-nourished, and possibly have suspect pedigrees.

Picking the Pet Puppy from the Litter
The most desirable age at which to collect your puppy is at about eight weeks old. By this age the breeder has taken care to have the puppy fully weaned and thoroughly wormed several times. If the puppy is left with his litter-mates much longer than this, he finds it more difficult to adjust to family life, as he becomes more dependant on doggie companionship.

If the puppy is to be a pet only, you should not be too swayed by one with a wistful look, but should consider your family requirements. For instance, do not pick the puppy who sits at the back of the kennel and surveys you all, if you have a family containing young children. For such a lively family you should choose one which bounds forward rapturously to greet all of you, and seems to have a very out-going temperament. Alternatively, should your family be composed of a peace and quiet-loving

Who could resist this group of youngsters? Photo: Diane Pearce

couple only, who want a sweet, quiet companion, then do not chose the puppy which appears to be "on the go" all the time. It will shatter your peace and exhaust you!

You must make sure that all the puppies look sound and healthy, do not have runny eyes or noses, and do not have a "pot-bellied" look, as this probably means digestive troubles. Above all, choose a puppy whose face and expression appeals most to you – remember you will live with this, hopefully, for well over a decade.

Golden puppies vary very much in colour, and the colour in the nest seldom remains the same in adult life, for they darken considerably over the years. The most accurate guide as to the final colour is that of the puppy's ears.

Choosing the Show Puppy

This is a much more difficult task than that of picking a pet puppy, for you have so much more to consider. First of all go to a kennel regularly producing show winners, and ask to watch the puppies playing about, and gradually sort out the two or three that look the most promising both in looks and temperament. In the show puppy you must have one which has a somewhat out-going personality, for a "drooping" show dog is at a great disadvantage. A multitude of faults can be hidden in the alert, active dog!

When you have seen the puppies running about, ask the breeder to put them individually on a table for you to look at, then go over them point by point, taking heed of the breeder's estimation of the puppy – for he has much more experience of little puppies than you have. Examine the bite, and look carefully at the head which, at eight weeks, should be nicely balanced with a fairly short foreface of good breadth and depth – the skull is not so important at this age – and should have a well-defined stop. A head lacking a good muzzle and stop at this age never develops them later in life.

Next, consider the bone in the front legs. This should be straight and strong, as a lightly-boned puppy will be the same when adult. So look for good bone and nicely rounded, tight feet. These can be somewhat deceptive on a puppy set-up on a table, as it is inclined to put its feet in the position which makes it feel the most secure, and this tends to make the feet look more open.

A good show prospect at 8 weeks old. Photo: Diane Pearce

The shoulder placement is very important at this age, for though bad shoulder placement can improve as the puppy grows and is reared properly, its litter-mate with the better shoulders at eight weeks will always score here. Make sure that there is good lay-back of the shoulder blade, and that they are not set too wide apart at the withers.

The next part of the anatomy to examine is the loin. This should be short and strong, giving a reasonably short body. The tail should be set on in line with the back; the stifles should be well-bent, and the hindquarters broad. The whole puppy should present a well-balanced appearance, without any exaggerations.

Choosing the Puppy for Work

If the puppy is required primarily as a gundog, the most important aspects to consider are those of character and temperament. The puppy chosen must be very bold and not afraid of any sudden loud noises or movements. It must be one which readily comes to see you and wishes to remain with you, rather than going off to explore on its own. Try getting the puppy's attention and throw

An early show winner. Photo: Thomas Fall

something a short distance, when hopefully, he will carry it. A puppy of this age which will pick up a thrown object is going to be easier to train than one showing no interest.

Taking the Puppy Home

When you have chosen your puppy, the breeder will issue you with his pedigree and Kennel Club Registration papers, providing these have been received by him. Do not buy a puppy unless assured that Registration documents have been applied for, as these are essential should you later decide to breed from, show or run your dog in Field Trials.

A diet sheet will also be issued to you. Keep strictly to this for the first week or two after getting the puppy home, as puppies' tummies are so easily upset by any change in feeding, and if care is not taken the puppy will soon have Diarrhoea. Ask the breeder about worming the puppy, for this should be done about every two weeks until it is three months old. Ascertain whether or not he has been inoculated. This should be done with a Distemper, Hepatitis and Leptospirosis once at eight weeks, and the whole inoculation repeated at about twelve weeks old.

Once home, the puppy will probably feel very strange in his new surroundings, and will be tired after his journey. Offer him some food, take him in the garden to relieve himself, and then show him his bed. Do not leave him to his own devices at first, but stay with him to start the human–dog relationship as soon as possible.

Chapter 4

Puppy Rearing and Early Training

Housing
When you get your puppy home he must be given his own bed, where he knows he may rest quietly without disturbance, and this bed must be his own domain to which he may take his toys, and enjoy his own company for as long as he wishes. At first his bed may be a cardboard box, with a rug in the bottom, and this should be placed in a warm corner. As he grows he will need a larger bed, and I suggest the use of a canvas bed on a metal frame, a number of which are on the market. These are easy to clean and practically indestructable. Unfortunately, young Goldens have a penchant for chewing their beds, so those made of wickerwork, decorative as these may seem, are not advisable. It is not desirable to house one Golden on its own in a kennel, and anyone buying a Golden as a pet should be prepared to have it sharing their home day and night. This breed so rely on human companionship that I think it unkind to subject one dog alone to the confinement of kennel life.

Feeding
At eight weeks old the puppy's diet will comprise four meals a day, with one or two of these consisting of meat and cereal, and the others of milk and cereal. There are no hard and fast rules as to the timing of the meals, but they should be spaced equally during the day (which is generally at about four and a half hourly intervals). As stated earlier, you should follow the breeder's diet sheet absolutely at first, but after a few weeks you can introduce your own variations. Either fresh or tinned meat can be fed with equally good results. If one of the better brands of tinned meats is used, then it should not be necessary to add extra Vitamins and Calcium, as these are already added, and too much vitamins can be as harmful as too little. However, an inferior brand, or even fresh meat, will need the addition of Calcium, Vitamins A, B, D and E, together with various minerals.

A Golden Retriever puppy at 3½ months old

As the puppy grows, so the quantities it eats must be increased until at about three months old it should be having three meals a day consisting of:

1. 6 oz (170g) meat and cereal.
2. 6 oz (170g) meat and cereal.
3. Milk and cereal.

At this age he may be introduced to a marrow-bone (no other sort is suitable). This should first be held by you, as the dog gnaws on the other end. Puppies can be very possessive with bones and care should be taken when introducing these. Having held the bone, give it to him, then take it from him again, and immediately give it back to him, so that he learns that he can trust you not to deprive him of the very cherished possession – for a bone is a dog's best and most loved toy.

By the time he is six months old the meals can be reduced to two a day and the dog should be eating his full adult rations i.e. about 1 lb (½ Kg) meat and ¾ – 1 lb (375 – 500 gms) of cereal daily. Some puppies will even eat more biscuit meal than the quantities given above, without becoming too fat, and some will find it difficult to consume as much as this. The individual dog's needs must be pandered to as they vary so much.

When he reaches nine months old it is usual to cut his meals down to one a day, given at whatever time suits you best – but do keep regularly to the same time of day. He will still need the same quantity of food as was given at six months old, but this quantity is all given together in the one meal.

It is quite possible to vary the dog's diet if desired, by sometimes feeding fish or tripe instead of meat, and some dogs love the treat of bread rather than their own biscuit meal. Eggs and milk are also good additives occasionally.

Grooming

This should be commenced early in the puppy's life, and a daily session is advised. For a puppy a nylon hair brush is quite adequate, together with a metal comb. As the puppy grows a stiffer brush can be used until he is growing his adult coat, when a wire hound-glove is recommended.

Ch. Pippa of Westley, with 17 C.C.s is the breeds top winning bitch (whelped 1957). Photo: Sally Anne Thompson

House-Training

Commence his house-training as soon as you get him home, for it is far easier to do this before he develops any bad habits. Avoid, if possible, his "performing" in the house, by picking him up and taking him into the garden immediately he wakes up, after each meal, and at very frequent intervals throughout the day.

Puppies seem to need to "spend pennies" about every half hour, and do not wait until you see him looking for a spot on the carpet, but take him out before an accident becomes imminent. Go out with him, and stay out, until the desired event takes place, then praise him, and tell him what a good boy he is letting him go straight back into the house if he so desires. Do not scold him for making a puddle in the house unless you actually catch him in the act. This will only confuse him and do no good. Goldens are very easy to house-train if you are prepared to spend the time doing so, but you cannot expect a baby puppy to contain itself for too long, and they are frequently about four months old before they can go through the night.

Training to the Car

Most adult Goldens love the car and will make a dash to get in as soon as the door is opened, but, unfortunately, a lot of puppies suffer severe car-sickness. To help to overcome this, it is a good idea to take the youngster, but not until his inoculations are completed, for short rides, with good romps at the end of them, so that he begins to associate the car with something pleasurable. Even a short ride to collect the children from school is ideal, for he can meet other people and feel a happy atmosphere, and there is the excitement of the family being re-united.

When the puppy accepts the short rides happily, these can be lengthened, and soon he should be enjoying his second home – the family car. It is advisable always to have the dog wearing a collar with his address on, when he is in the car, in case of accidents. It is also advisable to confine the dog to the back of the car with a dog-guard.

Training the Puppy to be Obedient

The early lessons of obedience should start as soon as the puppy joins you. One of the first things to be taught should be the meaning of the word "No". To make this word mean something to him, it should only be used if one is prepared to enforce it, so do not use the word unless you know that you can make the dog stop what it is doing. Another equally important aspect of his early training is to get him to come to you when he is called, so he must learn his name as soon as possible.

The puppy should learn that to come to you is always a pleasurable experience so that, in the initial training, it is a good thing to have a tit-bit available, and when he comes to you reward him with this. Never call him if you feel his full attention is not on you and he may be disobedient. The essence of the "come" call is to make sure that it will be obeyed, particularly in the early stages. Wait before calling him until you are sure he will come – possibly only call him when he is actually on his way to you! Praise him when he does come and give him the tit-bit.

Some dogs can be exasperating if not trained properly, and can completely ignore your calling. When eventually he does come, if he has disobeyed you, again praise him – even if he has not returned to you for half an hour! To scold him is to cause mistrust in him and he will be very wary of coming to you at all in the future. Goldens as a breed are very sensitive to correction and it should seldom be necessary to do more than scold them. However, should they repeatedly disobey you then a good shaking is the most effective way of chastisement.

A fine study of a Golden Retriever. Photo: Thomas Fall

A one year old dog—Camrose Luciue. Photo: C. M. Cooke

Training to the Leash
For the puppy destined to be the family pet it is essential for him to be accustomed to the collar and leash at an early age. Firstly, get him used to wearing a collar in the house – some puppies resent this very much at first, and spend all their time scratching at it. However, they soon become used to wearing it, and accept it as part of their life. Next, attach the leash to the collar, either in the house or the garden, and try to get the puppy to follow you as you move away from him. If he shows any reluctance to do this, have a tit-bit at the ready, and hold it in front of his nose to encourage him. As soon as he does what you want, even if he only moves a few feet, give him the tit-bit and lots of praise. Repeat the process until you have him happily trotting at your side. Do not take him out of his own environment until he is quite unconcerned about the collar and leash.

Heel Training
Another useful lesson for a growing Golden is that of walking to heel – this obviates the infuriating habit of a grown dog pulling its owner all over the place. If the puppy is to be a family dog, it is advisable to start teaching him heel work whilst he is still in his early days of going for walks; for the dog destined for work with the gun, it is not necessary to start until six–eight months.

Six appealing puppies of 8 weeks old—adorable, but they can also be a handful to cope with! Photo: Diane Pearce

Providing the dog is not very headstrong, a nylon slip-leash will be sufficient, but should he need firmer handling, then a metal choke-chain will be necessary. Place this on the dog's neck so that the leash slackens easily, and with the dog on your left side give a slight jerk on the leash and start walking away from him, whilst delivering the command "Heel". Should the puppy get ahead of you, jerk the leash backwards, repeating the word "Heel", and when he complies with this order, praise him. Should he lag behind, jerk the leash forward, repeating the command "Heel", and encourage him by talking to him as this helps to keep his concentration on you. Soon the action of the jerk on the leash is associated with the word "Heel", and short lessons of about 10 minutes a day should soon make it unnecessary to give the tug on the leash.

Sit and Stay
This is a very useful obedience exercise for either the pet dog or for any other, as it instils in him the basic rule that when told to sit, he does so, and stays there until told he may move.

Put the slip-leash on him and give the command "Sit", at the same time pushing his hindquarters on to the ground, to enforce the command. Hold him down, repeating the "Sit" command for a while, until he will stay there on his own. Should he attempt to get up say "No, sit" very firmly, and tush him down again. Make him stay in this position for increasing lengths of time, so that you know that he will obey. When you decide he can get up – not when he decides – call his name, and allow him to get up, and make a great fuss of him.

Soon he will have learned the "Sit" lesson, so now you must

start on the "Stay". This involves your placing him in the sitting position, still keeping him on the leash and walking a few paces backwards away from him, whilst raising your hand in front of him and saying "Stay". At any attempt on his part to get up, go straight back to him, make him sit once more, and repeat the "Stay" exercise. Considerable time and patience may be required before you reach the stage of being able to walk away without the dog following you. Gradually increase the distance you walk away from him, and each time he gets up, put him firmly down on the original spot. Thus he will eventually learn to do what is required.

At first when you have been successful, and he has remained sitting whilst you have gone the required distance from him, do not make the mistake of calling him up to you. This makes the dog much more ready to "break". Instead, walk back to him and praise him whilst allowing him to get up. Later, as he becomes more reliable, you can recall him to you, and suitably reward him with your praise.

Exercise
From eight weeks old puppies need plenty of free exercise, so that they may grow up strong and healthy in body and temperament.

A Golden Retriever at one year old. Photo: Diane Pearce

The family dog is usually required to go out for walks at far too early an age, and I would never advise long leash-walks at under the age of about four months. It is much better to take the puppy for a romp off the leash, providing the facilities are available, until its bones begin to harden.

At about four months of age, fifteen minutes a day on the road is quite sufficient. This can gradually be increased, but until the puppy is six months old it should not be subjected to long walks. From six months, it should have about forty minutes a day road work and about thirty minutes of romping on grass, away from home, and this suffices also for an adult Golden.

Do not expect him to exercise himself whilst you sit down and watch him. He will prefer your companionship and will stay with you rather than running about on his own. As I said earlier, if you do not want to exert yourself too much, Goldens are very happy for you to throw something for them to retrieve, and this is excellent exercise for them.

Chapter 5

General Care of the Adult Golden

Providing the basic requirements of good housing, good food and regular exercise are kept to, your Golden should cause you little trouble. As these aspects have all beeen dealt with in the previous chapter, I do not need to touch on these again. Other tips on the regular care of your dog are listed below.

Grooming
This should be done each day, particularly after exercise, to remove any burrs or tangles from the coat. To make a Golden's coat look its best, the brushing should be done with a wire hound-glove, which makes the coat shine, and improves its condition. This should be used so that the wire bends with the way the coat grows, so that the skin is not harmed. Finish off with a fairly wide-toothed metal comb. This is essential for the long feathering on front legs, trousers and tail.

Bathing
Goldens do not need bathing very often, if regularly groomed, but they do have a great love of muddy puddles, and in fact, of mud in general, so it is occasionally necessary to resort to bathing. For this you require a good quality shampoo, and, if this is a dog shampoo, ensure that it contains an insecticide, as this will kill all pests, should the dog have these in his coat. He should have his coat thoroughly wetted, then the shampoo rubbed in well, then all rinsed out very thoroughly. We find that the condition of the coat is very much improved if we finish with a conditioning lotion, similar to that used by ourselves. This must be rubbed into the coat and left there for several minutes, before being thoroughly rinsed out.

Drying
One of the easiest ways of drying the dog after bathing is by using a chamois leather. This very quickly gets all the surplus water out

of the coat, and is much preferable to the use of towels. Newspaper is another good thing to use to remove excess moisture from the coat, but this does tend to leave printer's ink on it.

These days many people have hair-dryers which are excellent to use when all the surplus moisture has been removed. Take care not to let the coat become too dry before combing it into place, as a Golden rough-dried will probably have its coat sticking up in spikes.

Inoculations

For health protection the dog must have regular annual booster injections against Distemper, Hepatitis and Leptospirosis. He will have had his first injections completed by about three months, and these must be renewed every twelve months until he is at

Sh. Ch. Gyrima Ariadne. Photo: Diane Pearce

Sh. Ch. Camrose Matilda, seen at 8½ years old. Photo: Diane Pearce

least eight years old. The Leptospirosis injections should be continued each year even after that age.

Worming

Your Golden should have been wormed regularly as a puppy, and should be rewormed for round worms every six months after that. Many owners assume that as they see no signs of the dog having worms he is free from these parasites. This is not so, and he would indeed be very badly infested with worms before he passed these in his motions without a worming medicine being administered.

The tablets should be bought from your yet, and to give the correct dosage, he will require to know the dog's weight. Dogs can pick up various other types of worms, such as Hook Worms, Tape-worms and such but they should not be dosed against these parasites unless definite evidence is found that they have them. Should the dog appear to be losing weight, and seem to be choosy about his food, it is advisable to have a sample of his motions tested to find out if this is caused by worms or some other complaint.

41

Sh. Ch. Stenbury Seasonnet in show stance

External Parasites

The most usual of these are fleas and lice, but there are various types of tiny mites which can be harboured in the coat without being seen. There is no reason why a dog should have any of these parasites, as they are easily removed, and no type of livestock should be tolerated on the dog as they can cause him much distress, and dog fleas transmit tapeworm to the animal.

In order to clean the coat of parasites there are many insecticides on the market in both powder and spray form, but you must make sure that the one you are using is for the correct insect. They should be worked well into the coat, left there for a while, and then brushed out. It is important to follow exactly the instructions on the container. Your vet can provide you with excellent "dips" for this purpose, and these are probably the most reliable ways of making quite sure that all the insects are killed. Again, the instructions must be carefully followed. Whether powder or bath is resorted to, the dog should be re-treated at about a 10 day interval to ensure any eggs which may have hatched out are killed.

Minor Ailments which might be Encountered

Impacted Anal Glands These glands are situated at either side of the anus, and sometimes become overfilled with secretion. This causes irritation, and the dog rubs its rear on the ground, and constantly licks itself. This can easily be alleviated by allowing your vet to squeeze the secretion out with his finger and thumb.

Canker This appears as an intense irritation of the ear and causes the dog to shake its head and scratch the ear, or hold the head on one side. The condition is also recognisable by the internal canal containing a brownish-red discharge. Clean out the ear with a cotton-wool bud and insert a canker powder or lotion, according to the instructions, but always be very careful not to probe at the inner ear.

Another intense ear irritation can be caused by ear mites, usually caught from cats and, to clear up this condition it is necessary to get drops from your vet.

Diarrhoea There are varying causes of this, but if apparently just caused by eating something unsuitable, give the dog one tablespoon of Kaolin powder three times daily. Should the dog appear ill, however, consult your vet.

Eczema There are two types of this complaint, wet and dry. Wet eczema can be most unpleasant for it starts with little eruptions which soon exude moisture, and this causes the dog to bite and scratch the affected area, which soon begins to spread. It can appear anywhere on the body, but the most usual areas are at the base of the tail, on the tail, along the back, on the face and behind the ears. All the hair must be cut from the affected places and then calamine lotion applied three times daily.

With dry eczema the skin becomes reddened and there is a partial loss of hair and irritation. The most usually affected parts are the tummy, flanks and legs. A bath in a special shampoo should be used and this can be obtained from your vet.

Goldens mix well with all other breeds—they also adore cats. Photo: Diane Pearce

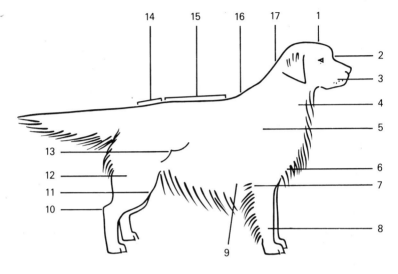

Glossary of terms

1 – Forehead	9 – Brisket
2 – Stop	10 – Hock
3 – Muzzle	11 – Stifle
4 – Throat	12 – Thigh
5 – Shoulder	13 – Loin
6 – Chest	14 – Croup
7 – Elbow	15 – Back
8 – Pastern	16 – Withers
	17 – Nape

Chapter 6

The Kennel Club Breed Standard and its Interpretation

Reproduced by kind permission of the Kennel Club

The Kennel Club Standard is given in full here, and it stands as a guide to breeders who endeavour to produce the typical Golden Retriever. To be typical, he must not only closely resemble the breed to which he belongs, but also be capable of doing the work for which he was bred, and have the correct temperament.

Many breeders endeavour to produce a dog which fulfils all the requirements of the Standard, but perfection in anything is very elusive, and this is certainly so in breeding dogs. I have been breeding, showing and judging dogs for many years, and I have yet to see the "perfect" specimen. Should anyone tell you "My dog is perfect, and I would not want him changed in any way", then you should advise him to take off his rosy-hued spectacles. Perfection is not for us mere mortals to achieve.

Kennel Club Standard
General Appearance. Should be of a symmetrical, active, powerful dog, a good level mover, sound and well put together, with a kindly expression, not clumsy or long in the leg.
Head and Skull. Broad skull, well set on a clean and muscular neck, muzzle powerful and wide, not weak-jawed, good stop.
Eyes. Dark and well set apart, very kindly in expression, with dark rims.
Ears. Well proportioned, of moderate size, and well set on.
Mouth. Teeth should be sound and strong. Neither overshot nor undershot, the lower teeth just behind but touching the upper.
Neck. The neck should be clean and muscular.
Forequarters. The forelegs should be straight with good bone. Shoulders should be well laid back and long in the blade.
Body. Well-balanced, short coupled, and deep through the heart. Ribs deep and well sprung.
Hindquarters. The loins and legs should be strong and.muscular,

with good second thighs and well bent stifles. Hocks well let down, not cow-hocked.

Feet. Round and cat-like, not open or splay.

Tail. Should not be carried too gay nor curled at the tip.

Coat. Should be flat or wavy with good feathering, and dense water-resisting undercoat.

Colour. Any shade of gold or cream, but neither red nor mahogany. The presence of a few white hairs on chest permissible. White collar, feet, toes or blaze should be penalised. Nose should be black.

Weight and Size. The average weight in good hard condition should be: Dogs 70 – 80 lbs (32 – 37 Kgs); Bitches 60 – 70 lbs (27 – 32 Kgs); Height at shoulder: Dogs 22 – 24 ins (55·88 – 60·96 cms); Bitches 20–22 ins (50·80–55·88 cms).

Interpretation
As the Standard is very short, and gives only a very rough idea of the desired conformation, I will enlarge on this.

General appearance
The Standard requires that the dog should present a symmetrical picture i.e. one which is in complete balance. Balance is achieved

A Golden poses with his friend, a Black and Tan Terrier. Photo: Diane Pearce

by having all the various parts of the anatomy relating well to each other. The length of the leg and the length of the body must be in proportion to one another, as must be the length of the neck and hindquarters. A dog with a long neck, short legs and short back is not well-balanced, neither is one with too short a neck and a long body and long legs. True symmetry is achieved when the dog forms a "square" when measured from front foot to withers, from withers to root of tail, from there to the hind foot, and back again to front foot.

Goldens were specifically bred as gundogs, and therefore, as the Standard says, they should be active and powerful. Naturally, activity must be encountered in the dog at work, and he must be powerfully enough built to carry heavy game, and be able to jump whilst doing so. He must have sufficient bone and substance to be able to endure a hard day's work, but must not be "cloddy", which would make him too cumbersome. Nor must he be "weedy", which would defeat the object, which is a dog with staying power, as well as speed. Quality is the desired attribute, lying half-way between the two extremes, and is some indefinable thing which must appear in all high-class pedigree dogs; a combination of beauty and balance.

Head and Skull
Again, the head must be balanced. This means that the length and breadth of the skull must be in proportion with the length and breadth of the foreface. The length of the skull should about equal the length of the muzzle; it should be broad, but without coarseness, and should be slightly rounded. A flat skull gives a "foxy" look, and invariably has the ears set on too high whilst a skull which is too domed is also incorrect as this gives a "houndy" appearance with the ears set on too low, and invariably, too long.

The stop should be well-defined without being over-developed, and the frontal bones above the eyes should not be too prominent. The muzzle must be straight, without any sign of Roman nose or "dish-face", as in a Pointer. The correct foreface should be in

Stop too deep   Stop too shallow   Correct

Correct and faulty heads

Ch. Stolford Happy Lad. Photo: Diane Pearce

proportion to the skull in length, and should be broad and strong, with good depth. A snipey muzzle, or one which is lacking in depth, is quite untypical, as is a head showing wrinkle or frown.

Eyes
These should be dark brown and most expressive. The whole character of the dog shines out of his expression and the shape and colour of his eyes provides this. They should be round but not too prominent, nor set too deep into the head. Obliquely set or almond shaped eyes are not typical of the breed. The Standard allows the eye colour to match that of the coat, but does not permit it to be any shade of yellow – this is most objectionable.

Ears
The ears should just touch the edge of the eyes, when pulled forward, and should not be too thick in texture. If too long they are inclined to give a "houndy" look, and do not lie correctly against the face, but tend to fold. To be set on in the correct position, the top, inner edge of the ears should be roughly in line with the eyes.

Mouth

The correct bite of the Golden is when the front, top teeth just meet and overlap the upper edge of the bottom ones. The milk teeth come out at about four months of age, and it is only when the second teeth are fully grown that one can correctly assess the bite. When the dog is still a puppy the upper teeth generally overlap the bottom ones much more than in the adult dog, and this is how one likes a puppy's bite to be. If absolutely correct at six months old, he may well become somewhat "near" later on, as the bottom jaw grows on long after the second teeth are in place. A dog which is undershot is useless for show, but this should not be confused with misaligned teeth, which is not such a serious fault. It is very unusual to find a Golden which is overshot as an adult, in fact, I have never seen one.

Nose

This should be black, as a nose lacking true pigmentation detracts so much from the dog's expression. Many dogs lose the lovely black pigmentation during the winter, but this re-appears with the summer's sun. Bitches about to come into season can also lose the blackness from their noses, but this invariably returns when they are nursing their puppies. Some judges penalise a brownish nose, but, personally, I think it would have to detract very much from the expression before I would do so. A few Goldens do have pinkish coloured noses, and this is very undesirable.

Neck and Shoulders

These two parts of the body are interdependent, and without a correct shoulder lay-back it is very unlikely that one would get a correct length of neck. Too many judges these days have no idea of correct shoulder formation, and time and again one reads a critique of a dog which says "Good neck and shoulders", when one knows that it has the most upright shoulder placement imaginable.

There are a great number of Goldens at the present time which have incorrect shoulders, and it is quite true to say, as told to me years ago by the great all-rounder judge, Mr. Bill Siggers, and as quoted here from the book of R. H. Smythe, *The Anatomy of Dog Breeding*, "It would be almost impossible to think of any feature transmitted by dog or bitch to their progeny with greater certainty than faulty necks and shoulders".

The neck should be clean and muscular, which means that it should be free from excessive throatiness, which detracts much from the dog's appearance, and it must have muscularity, in order to allow the dog to carry heavy weights over long distances.

The Standard does not state that good length of neck is desirable, but this must be so if the dog is to be balanced, when shoulders are required which are well laid back.

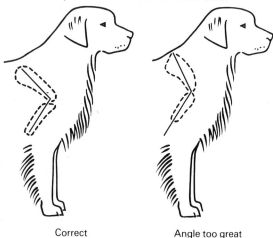

Correct   Angle too great

Correct and faulty shoulder blade placement

The scapula, or shoulder-blade, should be sloping, and the humerus, or upper arm, should be long and set at such an angle as to place the forelegs well under the body. The most desirable angulation, where these two bones meet, should be about 90 degrees. If these two bones are set at too wide an angle, then the placement of the shoulders becomes too upright, and this affects movement, for a dog with upright shoulders does not have the freedom of movement he should, and is likely to be one who moves with a "hackney" action, which is quite incorrect in a Golden (this is when the dog moves by lifting his front legs up very high).

The shoulder blades should not be too wide apart at the withers, and I consider the correct space is that which allows of two fingers being placed between them. There must be sufficient space between the blades to allow the dog to lower its head without these touching, for they will converge with this particular movement. Shoulder blades which are too far apart are invariably accompanied by upright positioning, and are also often accompanied by too much muscle, and this causes a "bossy" look.

These over-loaded shoulders are untypical for a Golden, which can live to old age with completely clean shoulders if they are correctly constructed. Here I instance my own Ch. Camrose Cabus Christopher, who was the greatest show dog of all times (winning 41 c.c.'s). He, at the age of 9½ when he died, still had beautifully clean shoulders, with no excess muscle on them, though he had every excuse to develop it, by being worked very hard throughout each shooting season.

Forelegs
The forelegs, looked at from the front, should be absolutely straight, with no turning out of the elbows or pasterns. A straight front is something which frequently accompanies good shoul-

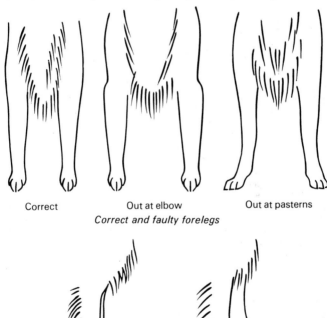

| Correct | Out at elbow | Out at pasterns |

Correct and faulty forelegs

| Correct | Down on pasterns |

Correct and faulty pasterns

51

A completely out-of-coat bitch illustrates the darkest colour permissible in the standard. Photo: Diane Pearce

ders. It can be achieved with a wide shoulder, but this invariably makes the dog somewhat out at elbow i.e. not having the elbows tucked well under the body. The bone in the front leg should be strong and round, giving a look of power, and enabling the working dog to carry its weight easily.

When looked at from the side, the front should also appear straight from elbow to foot, with no weakness or sloping of the pastern. The legs should be set well under the body when perpendicular with the ground.

Body
The body of the Golden should be well-proportioned and in balance. The Standard desires a short-coupled dog, and this is one which has a short loin – the loin is the space between the last rib and the pelvis. In order to fulfil his role in life as a dog of endurance, he must have a fairly long rib cage, to allow of full expansion of the lungs, and no over-crowding of the internal organs. This rib cage must also be fairly deep, giving the dog good depth of brisket, or making him "deep through the heart".

Without sufficient spring of rib, or breadth of rib cage, the dog would also be impeded in his various tasks, and a slab-sided dog looks weak and lacking in substance.

Some Goldens, as young dogs, do not fulfil these requirements in the breed Standard, for they are a slow-maturing breed, and up to the age of three often look lacking in body development through not having sufficient depth of body or spring of rib. It cannot be assumed that these faults will necessarily disappear as the dog matures, but the rather leggy immature pup can blossom into a top-class specimen at three years of age.

Top-line
The top-line of a Golden should be level from the withers to the tail-set, which point is omitted from the Standard, but expected by all breeders and judges. The dog which slopes from the shoulder to the croup has the appearance of a Setter, and the dog with a sloping croup and low-set tail is also incorrect in topline. The other fault of top-line is when the dog dips behind the shoulder and goes up again over the hindquarters. This is caused by a weak back.

Hindquarters
The Standard says that the loins should be strong, and this means well-covered with muscle, thus giving an appearance of the whole body being held together without too much tuck-up under, or weediness across, the loin. A dog which is too long in the loin can appear weak, for he will have the muscles spaced out over a larger area. The hindlegs are also required to have good muscular development across the thighs and second thighs. Without this the dog appears narrow across his hindquarters. This muscle can

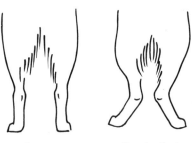

Correct   Cow-hocked
Correct and faulty hindlegs

be developed by the correct type of exercise, and is essential in a healthy, strong dog.

Looked at from behind, the quarters should look broad and have the muscle showing. The dog should have hind legs which are straight, and show no sign of the hocks either turning in or out. The weakness of hocks turning in is called "cow-hocks", and is most undesirable. It is sometimes an inherited condition, or it can be caused by incorrect feeding or environment. Correct exercise in the young dog can, sometimes, improve the hind movement.

Stifles

The stifles should be well-bent to enable both ends to move in harmony, for, if the shoulders are correctly placed, so must there be sufficient bend of stifles to enable the length of stride which will be required for balance.

It is also necessary for the dog to have good angulation between the pelvis and the femur. This is correct when the angulation is similar to that of the shoulder and upper arm, and when the angle between the femur and tibia (stifle) is not too great. This enables the dog to have a good turn of stifle.

The well-formed hindquarter enables the dog to have a long, free stride when moving, providing of course, that his forehand conformation is correct. Straight stifles make the dog move stiltedly, and without freedom. This is sometimes called "tied" movement. Over-angulation would be undesirable in the Golden, for any exaggeration would cause difficulty in balance of movement, and could only be compensated for in a long-bodied dog.

Croup

The croup should not slope, but be level with the back, and the tail should be set on in line with it. A sloping croup is caused by incorrect hindquarter construction, and often accompanies straight stifles.

Feet

The feet should be round and cat-like, and should not be too large. Good feet are also well-knuckled and should not be open or splay. Open feet can be improved by exercise on hard ground, which wears down the claws, but really good feet are bred in the dog.

Tail

The tail should be set on level with the back, and should be just long enough to reach the hock. It should be carried on a straight line with the back, with no sign of a curl at the end. A tail correctly carried adds much to the balance of the dog. The Standard allows

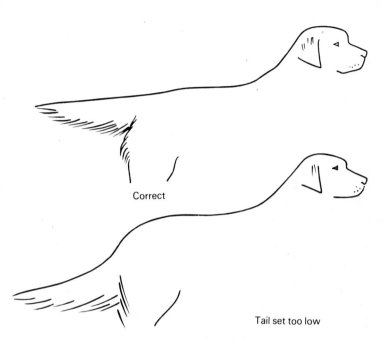

Correct

Tail set too low

Correct and faulty tail sets

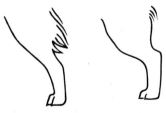

Stifle too straight   Correct

Correct and faulty stifles

Flat foot   Correct

Correct and faulty feet

of it being carried slightly higher than the back, but this does detract from the overall picture. It should never be carried over the back, nor tucked between the legs. The underside of the tail should be profusely covered with feathering, and this should be trimmed tidily if the dog is to be shown.

Coat
The coat of the Golden is one of the beautiful features of the breed, and it is useless to enter one in the showring which has undergone a moult, and is lacking its full plumage. The coat can be either straight or wavy and must have a dense undercoat. The hair is fairly long on the body and should not be too soft and silky nor too harsh in texture.

It is usual for the male to grow a heavy ruff round the neck (which must be carefully trimmed for the showring) and both sexes have long feathering on the back of the front legs, along the tummy, on the underside of the tail and on the trousers.

Colour
Goldens frequently commence life shades lighter than they are eventually. Puppies which appear very cream-coloured at eight weeks old often become a deep, mid-gold in adult life. The colour

Int. Ch. Camrose Evenpatrol C.D., T.D. (Berm.), just one of many Camrose Champions. Photo: Diane Pearce

of the ear is the safest guide as to the shade which a puppy will finish up. The Standard allows the coat colour to be any shade of gold or cream but excludes the very dark shades of red or mahogany. These very dark colours are not often encountered these days, and very few Goldens should ever be penalised for colour. Some judges still persist in excluding cream dogs from their awards, because they think of them as white. I would say that it is very unusual to have one which could be called white. Having owned very pale cream Goldens, and white cats, there has been no resemblance between the two colours. There is no correct colour in the Golden Retriever, all, except the very dark red ones, are acceptable and desirable. In fact the varying shades are one of the features which make them so attractive. One wishes judges would read the Standard and not make these particular comments, thus showing their lack of knowledge of the breed.

Weight and Size
Weights are clearly given in the Standard, but are only the average expected, and must vary very much from dog to dog. The heavier boned ones of good size, and in correct show condition, are going to weigh far more than the top weight given for their sex. Ch. Camrose Cabus Christopher was a dog of about 23¼ ins (59·8cm) and he weighed about 88 lbs. (40 kgs).

There is a terrific variation in the size allowed between the smallest bitch and the largest dog. A difference of 4 ins (10 cm) would look incredible, and actually, very few bitches are less than 21 ins (52 cm), and very few dogs are over 23½ ins (60 cm).

For me the ideal bitch size is about 21½ ins (53 cm). I think there are a lot of oversized bitches in the showring, but the dogs never come near the top size-limit. So many of today's dogs are nearer the 22 – 22½ ins (54·5 – 56 cm) mark, and I do not think this is a trend to be encouraged. To look really masculine, a dog should be considerably bigger than his female counterpart; mid-way between the Standard is ideal for a dog – 23 ins (58·8 cm).

Movement
For correct movement the Golden should move both his forelegs and backlegs straight and level, without any turning in or out. The lateral movement should present one of a long, free stride, with legs being picked up and flexed, rather than swinging, and there should be no sign of "hackney" action in front. The action seen from in front, should be of all the pads of the front feet touching the ground together, so that there is no turning inwards. From behind, the dog should not turn his hocks inwards, but they too should move in a straight line.

Chapter 7

Breeding

The Brood Bitch

Before starting on a breeding project you must carefully select your future brood bitch. This must be done with her parentage in mind, as well as her own attributes and faults being considered. One must also ensure that she and her immediate family are free from hereditary defects.

It is advisable to select her from a well-established strain which has already proved its worth, by consistently producing winners, either in the showring or the Field, according to which sphere you are hoping to cater for. It must be stressed that pedigree study is most helpful when you are selecting her, as she must come from a line of good winners, and not just be haphazardly bred from a mixture of out-crosses. A fairly strongly line-bred bitch is much more likely to reproduce the good points of the strain than one which has varying lines in her pedigree.

You must start with the best possible bitch you can afford, for a mediocre one is not likely to produce anything outstanding, even if mated to the best stud dog available. Some of the puppies may be better than their dam, but the proof of really good breeding can only be claimed when most of the litter are of high quality. This applies both to show and working stock, but for Field Trial bred puppies, instead of high quality insert good training potential.

When the brood bitch is chosen with a show career in mind for her puppies, she should conform as closely as possible to the breed Standard, and have no glaring faults. She should have the desired out-going, intelligent and loving temperament, and certainly not be of a nervous disposition.

If the puppies are destined to be workers, then it is not necessary that the dam be so near to the ideal in conformation. It is far more important that she is of very high intelligence, is biddable, and retrieves to hand speedily, and with a soft delivery. She should also be persistent in her hunting, be prepared to face the thickest cover, and have lots of endurance.

Two differing heads and coat colour variations are seen in these Goldens.
Photo: Diane Pearce

Choosing the Stud Dog

As a novice breeder, it is not advisable to purchase a stud dog of your own. Not only is this a difficult thing to do in Goldens, as most breeders will not part with a good stud dog, but it is not necessary, as you can have the use of the best dogs in the country for your bitch.

When deciding on the dog to use on your bitch, you must take into consideration the dog's pedigree, as well as his looks and temperament. If you hope to produce good quality puppies, then the dog chosen must be of good blood-lines, and preferably come from a strain which is line-bred to the bitch's line. Complete outcrosses should never be undertaken, unless absolutely essential, for they can be a complete disaster, and do not achieve anything.

The dog himself should be outstanding, for you cannot waste your good bitch on a dog which has not all the attributes you hope for in your puppies. He should conform as closely as possible to

59

the Standard, and should have everything you want him to offer. Never choose a stud dog that is exaggerated in any way, for these exaggerations tend to show in the puppies.

If your bitch is a little lacking in strength of head, do not choose the stud dog who is over-done in head. He should be one with as near perfect a head as possible.

Breeding Methods

Line-Breeding. This is the most usual way for novices to begin to found their own strain, and is the one most likely to give success.

When dogs with some common ancestor or ancestors are mated together, usually the mating of cousins, or uncle and niece, and others with more distant relationships, thus they are said to be line-bred.

When starting on such a breeding programme, you must ensure that the dog, or dogs, to be line-bred to, are themselves outstanding, for there is nó point in stamping in mediocrity, which is what will happen if inferior dogs are line-bred to. In both the showring and the Trial world, the hallmark of success, and an outstanding dog, is the magic word "Champion" or "Field Trial Champion" before the dog's name. One should not be prepared to line-breed to any Golden without a title in front of its name. This is the official recognition of its outstanding merit. Of course there are Champions and Champions. Some become good sires or

Sh. Ch. Grima Pipparetta. Photo: Diane Pearce

dams, and others do not have the genetic make up to stamp their own good qualities on their off-spring. This is one of the things which makes dog-breeding such an absorbing hobby, as everything can look excellent on paper, but no-one can tell what the end product will be. So, when choosing your Champions to line-breed to, make sure that they have been able to reproduce their own good qualities i.e. that they have been good winner-producers.

In-Breeding. This method is not one for the novice to try, for one must know absolutely all the faults and weaknesses behind the line, as with this method such faults will be brought to the fore.

In-breeding is referred to when matings take place between brothers and sisters, mothers to sons and fathers to daughters.

Out-Crossing. Again, this method is best left alone by the beginner, for success is so much less likely to be experienced. Dogs with unrelated pedigrees bring together so many different genes, that there can be no consistency in the litters produced. They will vary in type, and probably not have much resemblance to either of their parents.

Out-crossing should only be used when one has line-bred extensively, and you feel the time has come when improvement can only be reached by bringing fresh blood into the strain.

Matings

Golden bitches usually come into season for the first time between nine and twelve months of age, though some do go longer than this. They should not be mated on the first season, but have their first litter by about 18 months old.

As soon as the bitch comes into season, which is when the red discharge starts to show from the vagina, the owner of the stud dog should be notified, so that a suitable day for you both can be arranged on which the bitch can be taken for mating. The days most acceptable to Golden bitches for mating are from the tenth to the thirteenth days of their seasons. From the time the bitch comes into season until the time she finishes, about 21 days, a strict watch must be kept on her for she will have a great desire to get out and find a mate for herself.

On arrival at the stud dog's home, you will be asked to let her relieve herself, then she will be introduced to her mate, both dogs being kept on leashes at first. If your bitch shows no sign of aggression towards the dog he will be released and will start to flirt with her. Providing she is ready for mating she will then start to flirt with him, and when he has made sufficient advances to her, and he is sure that she will not attempt to snap at him, he will mount her. By this time she should be standing with hind-legs stiffened, tail turned upwards and held to one side, and she should be raising her vulva to aid the dog to penetrate. If, however, the bitch tries to snap at the dog, but at the same time appears to be ready, by turning her tail, the stud dog's owner will wish to tape the bitch's nose, to avoid the dog being snapped at.

The owner of the bitch will now be asked to hold her bitch's collar securely whilst the dog's owner supports the bitch under the loin. Sometimes the dog will mount the bitch several times before getting in the correct position to penetrate, and if difficulty is encountered, the owner of the dog should discover if he is working too high or too low. If he should be working too low, which frequently happens, the bitch should be placed with head facing down a slight slope in the ground, thus raising her hindquarters. If this slight adjustment works the dog will be able to penetrate, and will ride the bitch until his penis completely swells and he "ties", this is when a successful mating has taken place and the two animals are locked together. When tied, the dog will drop his front legs off the bitch, and soon will wish to turn.

Sh. Ch. Nortonwood Faunus. Photo: Anne Roslin-Williams

Ch. Camrose Fabius Tarquin (whelped 1975). Photo: Diane Pearce

This position is the natural one for dogs when mating, and is when the dog lifts one of his hindlegs completely over the bitch's back, thus enabling him to stand back to back with her. The tie can last for 10 minutes up to an hour or more, but most usually for about 15–20 minutes.

After the mating the bitch should immediately be returned to the car, so that she avoids spending a penny, and should be left to rest for a while before the homeward journey is undertaken. The dog can well be left to his own devices, but it is not advisable to return him to other males immediately, in case of jealousy.

The owner of the bitch will be asked to pay the stud fee immediately after the mating, and it is customary for the stud dog owner to offer a free service, should the bitch not prove to be in whelp – though this is not obligatory, as the fee is paid for the actual service.

It is most important that the bitch should be kept away from all

MATED JANUARY	DUE TO WHELP MARCH	MATED FEBRUARY	DUE TO WHELP APRIL	MATED MARCH	DUE TO WHELP MAY	MATED APRIL	DUE TO WHELP JUNE	MATED MAY	DUE TO WHELP JULY	MATED JUNE	DUE TO WHELP AUGUST	MATED JULY	DUE TO WHELP SEPTEMBER	MATED AUGUST	DUE TO WHELP OCTOBER	MATED SEPTEMBER	DUE TO WHELP NOVEMBER	MATED OCTOBER	DUE TO WHELP DECEMBER	MATED NOVEMBER	DUE TO WHELP JANUARY	MATED DECEMBER	DUE TO WHELP FEBRUARY
1	5	1	5	1	3	1	3	1	3	1	3	1	2	1	3	1	3	1	3	1	3	1	2
2	6	2	6	2	4	2	4	2	4	2	4	2	3	2	4	2	4	2	4	2	4	2	3
3	7	3	7	3	5	3	5	3	5	3	5	3	4	3	5	3	5	3	5	3	5	3	4
4	8	4	8	4	6	4	6	4	6	4	6	4	5	4	6	4	6	4	6	4	6	4	5
5	9	5	9	5	7	5	7	5	7	5	7	5	6	5	7	5	7	5	7	5	7	5	6
6	10	6	10	6	8	6	8	6	8	6	8	6	7	6	8	6	8	6	8	6	8	6	7
7	11	7	11	7	9	7	9	7	9	7	9	7	8	7	9	7	9	7	9	7	9	7	8
8	12	8	12	8	10	8	10	8	10	8	10	8	9	8	10	8	10	8	10	8	10	8	9
9	13	9	13	9	11	9	11	9	11	9	11	9	10	9	11	9	11	9	11	9	11	9	10
10	14	10	14	10	12	10	12	10	12	10	12	10	11	10	12	10	12	10	12	10	12	10	11
11	15	11	15	11	13	11	13	11	13	11	13	11	12	11	13	11	13	11	13	11	13	11	12
12	16	12	16	12	14	12	14	12	14	12	14	12	13	12	14	12	14	12	14	12	14	12	13
13	17	13	17	13	15	13	15	13	15	13	15	13	14	13	15	13	15	13	15	13	15	13	14
14	18	14	18	14	16	14	16	14	16	14	16	14	15	14	16	14	16	14	16	14	16	14	15
15	19	15	19	15	17	15	17	15	17	15	17	15	16	15	17	15	17	15	17	15	17	15	16
16	20	16	20	16	18	16	18	16	18	16	18	16	17	16	18	16	18	16	18	16	18	16	17
17	21	17	21	17	19	17	19	17	19	17	19	17	18	17	19	17	19	17	19	17	19	17	18
18	22	18	22	18	20	18	20	18	20	18	20	18	19	18	20	18	20	18	20	18	20	18	19
19	23	19	23	19	21	19	21	19	21	19	21	19	20	19	21	19	21	19	21	19	21	19	20
20	24	20	24	20	22	20	22	20	22	20	22	20	21	20	22	20	22	20	22	20	22	20	21
21	25	21	25	21	23	21	23	21	23	21	23	21	22	21	23	21	23	21	23	21	23	21	22
22	26	22	26	22	24	22	24	22	24	22	24	22	23	22	24	22	24	22	24	22	24	22	23
23	27	23	27	23	25	23	25	23	25	23	25	23	24	23	25	23	25	23	25	23	25	23	24
24	28	24	28	24	26	24	26	24	26	24	26	24	25	24	26	24	26	24	26	24	26	24	25
25	29	25	29	25	27	25	27	25	27	25	27	25	26	25	27	25	27	25	27	25	27	25	26
26	30	26	30	26	28	26	28	26	28	26	28	26	27	26	28	26	28	26	28	26	28	26	27
27	31	27	May 1	27	29	27	29	27	29	27	29	27	28	27	29	27	29	27	29	27	29	27	28
28	Apl. 1	28	2	28	30	28	30	28	30	28	30	28	29	28	30	28	30	28	30	28	30	28	Mar 1
29	2	29	3	29	31	29	July 1	29	31	29	31	29	30	29	31	29	Dec 1	29	31	29	31	29	2
30	3	—	—	30	June 1	30	2	30	Aug 1	30	Sept 1	30	Oct 1	30	Nov 1	30	2	30	Jan 1	30	Feb 1	30	3
31	4	—	—	31	2	—	—	31	2	—	—	31	2	31	2	—	—	31	2	—	—	31	4

Gestation table showing when a bitch is due to whelp

64

dogs until the end of her season, for it is possible for her to get mated to another dog, and occasionally a dual conception takes place i.e. the bitch may already have conceived to the original mate, and if ovulation is still taking place, she may also conceive to the second dog, and it would not be possible to make sure which puppies belonged to either of the two matings. Should this happen, or should she get out at any time during the season and choose her own mate, she should be taken to the vet within 24 hours of the unwanted mating for an injection. This should bring her into full season again, but should get rid of any unwanted puppies! Needless to say the bitch must not be mated until her next season.

Care of the In-whelp Bitch

The bitch must be kept from all other suitors after mating until she is completely out of season. Then she may resume her normal life and no special care need be taken of her until she is about four weeks in whelp, apart from worming her soon after mating, and again two weeks later.

The first visible signs of her pregnancy are the reddening and enlarging of her teats and the swelling of her sides just below the loins. These definite signs do not appear until about the fifth or sixth week after mating. Occasionally, earlier than this, the bitch will become difficult over her food, and may sometimes appear to start taking care of herself.

After the first four weeks, her meat ration should be increased and she should be given additional Vitamins and Calcium. It is also useful to add an egg or two to the diet and some milk, but these are not essential. On a diet such as this the bitch should be in good condition and ready for her whelping about 63 days after the mating. She should be allowed to use her own instincts, which will tell her how much exercise she should take, and she should not be forced to do anything too strenuous. She must have exercise, but within reason, to keep her muscles in good tone.

As the gestation period draws to its completion, and the bitch becomes heavier, she will probably start to get very uncomfortable, so it may become necessary to divide her usual meal into two, with about 12 hours between, so that the bulk is divided up.

About 10 days before the bitch whelps, the puppies start to move, and if you watch her carefully, when she is lying on her side, the movement can be seen, only slightly at first, but as the whelping day draws nearer the puppies become more active and the movement easier to detect.

Bitches vary in the timing of their whelpings, some being very punctual and starting to produce their families on the 63rd day. Some may do so several days before expected, and yet others several days late. Providing the bitch is eating well, and going about her daily routine without showing any signs of distress, then do not worry if she is up to four days late. After this time it is as well to get your vet to see that all is well.

One always hopes that the puppies will not arrive too many days prematurely, for there is less chance of their survival if from 5–7 days early – though we have had perfectly healthy litters born a week too soon.

The Whelping Quarters
The place where the bitch is to have her puppies should be prepared well in advance, so that all is well should she surprise you with an early whelping. If she is used to living in the house, and you have suitable accommodation for her, she will be happier having her family in her own surroundings, for the first week or two.

If she is to whelp in a kennel or shed, then this must be one which is draught-proof, for baby puppies need a temperature of about 80 degrees for the first day or two. Newly born puppies are

A very light-coloured variation of the Golden. Photo: Sally Anne Thompson

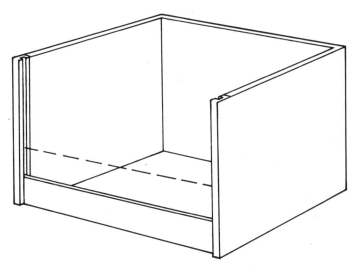

A typical whelping box

very subject to hypothermia, so no effort must be spared to keep them warm.

You will require a whelping box, which should be about 3½ ft – 4 ft (1 – 1·2 m) square, and have sides and back which are about 2 ft (61 cm) high, to help keep out the draughts. The front should be constructed of a piece of wood about 9 ins (23 cm) high, which can be taken out, or added to, as time goes on. The box can be constructed of ply wood, which is easy to clean, and we find this quite suitable for taking to pieces and disinfecting between litters; the pieces are fastened together with bolts and wing nuts.

Goldens are very careful with their baby puppies, and we have never experienced any clumsiness, or over-laying of puppies, so have never found it necessary to use a "pig-rail", but many breeders do, and if you are not sure of your bitch, it is probably better to be on the safe side. This pig-rail comprises a piece of wood, somewhat like a broom handle, which is fixed round the two sides and back of the box, about 5 ins (13 cm) from the bottom and 5 ins (13 cm) from the sides. This enables the puppies to get underneath, and stops the bitch from crushing them.

As warmth is so essential for the puppies, it is necessary to

Treunair Treubach, at 7 years of age, returning with dummy and over water to owner

have an infra-red lamp suspended above the box, as near central as is possible. It should be about 3 ft (91 cm) above the box, and the power of the lamp will vary according to the time of year. The lamp must be of the dull emitter type, and not one of the glass bulbs which are dangerous, for they sometimes explode. For the actual whelping we always have a great deal of heat, and the lamp used is 400 watts. In addition to this we also have other heating in the kennel of about 1000 watts. Later, if the weather is warm enough, we decrease the lamp to 300 watts, but not until the puppies are several days old, and, in the warmer parts of the year to 200 watts. Of course, as the puppies grow and become more active, the heat is discontinued, but except on hot days we like the puppies to have this until they are about three weeks old.

Whelping

For use during the whelping you will need a lot of newspapers, and the box should be lined with several layers, and added to, or changed if possible during the whelping. Other necessities for the great event are towels, soap and hot water, warm milk for the bitch and brandy – for either owner or bitch! A Thermos flask of tea or coffeee is helpful for the owner's consumption during the whelping, for this can be a very lengthy and tiring proceeding.

Most bitches give one some warning that their puppies are about to be born by becoming restless and starting to pant, asking to go out, and digging holes frantically. This can go on for as long as 24 hours, but might just last for an hour or so before labour starts. More usually this first stage lasts for about 12 hours.

When the second stage is reached the bitch will become more agitated, and will start to strain, which is when labour actually begins. At this stage she should be taken to her whelping quarters – before this she will not feel inclined to settle there alone – and you should be prepared to stay with her throughout the whelping.

At first the strains will not be very violent and she will have about 3 or 4 strains one after the other, then will rest for about 10 minutes before the next strains follow. During this time she will probably be sitting up and panting, and will periodically want to dig up the papers in her box. Gradually the strains will become stronger and more frequent, until the final expulsive strains start. This is when the first puppy reaches the vagina and should soon be born. At about this time, or very much earlier, she may begin to lose a vast amount of lightly-coloured clear discharge. This is when the water-bag breaks and means that things are really under way.

The bitch can be in labour for only about 15 minutes, or up to 2

This picture shows the two extremes of colours permitted by the Standard. Photo: Diane Pearce

hours, before the first puppy is born, but she should not be allowed to keep on straining for longer than two hours. If no puppy appears, veterinary advice should be called for.

The puppy should be born head first, and some bitches panic when this appears at the mouth of the vagina, and stop straining for a while. However, let nature take its course, and soon the downward pushing will make the straining start again, and in the meantime, the puppy is in no danger, for it is safely encased in its own bag. Gradually the rest of the puppy will be delivered with its own afterbirth attached, and the bitch should immediately start to pull the membrane encasing the puppy away from its head, thus enabling it to breathe. She will then proceed to eat the afterbirth and break the umbilical cord. However, should she fail to take any interest in the puppy at first, you must break the bag, for without air the puppy will soon die. Sever the cord about an inch from the puppy's body and this is best done with the finger nails, gradually breaking the cord by pulling towards the puppy. It is most essential that the bitch be allowed to eat the afterbirths as these provide her with the correct nutriments she requires after whelping.

Frequently puppies are born the wrong way round, and appear feet first. This is no unusual occurrence and the birth proceeds as quickly as in the normal way, providing the bag has not been burst. Should this breach birth have happened, and the feet start to appear from the vulva, then the puppy is in danger of suffocation or becoming water-logged. The sooner the puppy can be extracted the better, and a little help can be given by holding the feet, and pulling gently with each strain the bitch gives. When born, and the afterbirth removed, the puppy will need rubbing vigorously to stimulate the breathing, and will require the water shaking out of its lungs.

When the first puppy has been delivered and cleaned up by the bitch she will probably take a little rest, but soon the panting will begin again, and another puppy will be on its way. She may go only 10 minutes from the time of one puppy's arrival and the commencement of the straining again, but this varies, and there may be a resting period of as much as 2 hours before the next arrival is on its way. It is quite usual for a litter of 8 Golden puppies to take as long as 8 hours to be born, or even longer.

It is difficult to tell when the bitch has had her last puppy, for one wonders whether, 2 hours after the birth of the last one, she is just resting or if all the puppies have been born. We have frequently decided that all is well, and left the bitch comfortably settled with her family, and found to our surprise, on our next visit to the kennel, that another puppy has been born!

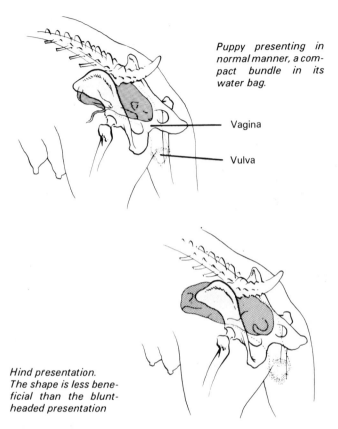

Puppy presenting in normal manner, a compact bundle in its water bag.

— Vagina

— Vulva

Hind presentation. The shape is less beneficial than the blunt-headed presentation

Occasionally the bitch will keep on straining for several hours after having the puppies, and this makes it very difficult to decide whether there is another puppy there, or if she is only straining on retained afterbirths. It is essential to have your vet check the bitch a few hours after the last puppy has been born, and to give an injection which ensures that the womb is cleared out and closed down, and also avoids any infection arising.

It is a good idea to give the bitch occasional drinks of warm milk during the whelping. No food will be required for some 12 hours after the birth of the family, for the mother still has plenty of nourishment from the consuming of the afterbirths.

71

Goldens have a penchant for digging and getting dirty! Photo: Diane Pearce

Care after whelping

When all is complete, get the bitch outside in order that she may relieve herself, and whilst she is out change her bedding, putting fresh layers of newspapers into the box. Leave her now to rest with the puppies and do not disturb her for a while.

For the next day her diet should be a light one of fish, milk and eggs given with cereal, but within 24 hours she may be given her normal diet, to which should be added as much liquid as she will drink, preferably milk. Some lactating bitches are unable to digest milk, so this must be watched, and if the motions do not firm up within 48 hours the milk should be stopped.

It is advisable to check the bitch's temperature for the first few days after whelping. The normal temperature should be 101·5F degrees, but it is quite usual for this to rise to 102·5F degrees for the first day or two. Should it go higher than this your vet should be consulted.

For the first few days the bitch will have a green discharge from the vulva, but this should gradually decrease. If this discharge becomes a pinky-yellow one, and becomes foul smelling, this indicates that the bitch has probably developed a womb infection, so your veterinary surgeon's help is needed.

Dew claws
There is no necessity to remove the dew claws from Golden puppies, and very few breeders do so – in fact, I have never had this done, and have never experienced any trouble later in life.

Dutch Dual Ch. Andy van Sparrenrode in a relaxed mood.

Chapter 8

Care of the Bitch and Puppies to Eight Weeks

Golden bitches often have large litters, we once had 16, but this is very unusual, and breeders sometimes wonder how many puppies their bitch can rear. Goldens can happily cope with 12 or 13 puppies, if the owner is prepared to supplement the feeding, and I would never consider having a healthy puppy put down. It is quite easy to bottle feed the puppies twice a day, with the aid of an ordinary baby's feeding bottle fitted with a premature teat which needs the hole in the end enlarging somewhat. This is done by heating a needle over a flame, then piercing the hole. The formula we use for this bottle feeding is a mixture of 2 parts evaporated milk and 1 part water. A litter of up to 10 puppies can easily be looked after by the bitch providing they are taught to lap at about 2½ weeks old.

Care of the Dam
A strict watch must be kept on the dam for the first few days after whelping, and any sign of her losing interest in her food, or becoming restless, should be regarded with suspicion. Any impending health disorder usually causes loss of appetite and a rise in temperature.

Her milk glands must be carefully watched for the first few days, as these can very easily become impacted and hard. Should you find any hardening or lumpiness in the glands, apply hot fomentations to the affected part. Having softened the glands somewhat, gentle massaging is helpful, and after this squeeze as much milk as possible out of the teats around the hardened glands. This treatment should be repeated at about 4-hourly intervals, until the glands return to normal.

Feeding the Bitch
I have given the feeding instructions for the first few days after

whelping in the previous Chapter, but as the days go on, and the puppies start to grow, the mother will need more and more food. For a bitch with puppies of about 2 weeks old, the average daily intake of food, divided into three meals, should be 3 lbs (1·4 kg) of meat and 2 lbs (·9 kg) of biscuit meal, plus all the milk she will take, and added Calcium and Vitamins. This amount of food daily will see her through the next weeks, and as you start to wean the puppies so the bitch's food can be decreased, if she finds these quantities too much.

For the first three weeks of the puppies' lives, unless the litter is a large one, there is little to be done for them, as the dam keeps them clean, by eating all their excretia.

Bedding
The bedding will become soiled, even though the bitch is cleaning up after the puppies, and this will need regularly changing. There

Ch. Brambletyne Carrock Fell of Daryock. Photo: Diane Pearce

Typical kind, alert head study of a dog, showing correct ear-set and shape.
Photo: Diane Pearce

are various types of bedding which can be used, but we find newspaper is very warm and absorbent. However, the puppies find it hard to grip on this with their feet, and probably the best type of bedding is either sacking or blankets. Straw, which can harbour lice, or wood wool, are not recommended as the bitch usually manages to move all this to the sides of the bed, and leaves the slippery, cold wood for her babes to lie on. Even if she does leave the wood wool in place, there is considerable danger of the puppies becoming entangled in it, or being pushed under it.

It may be necessary, when the puppies are about a week old, to shorten the claws on the front feet, as these can make the milk glands very tender – though with the profuse coats which Goldens have, this does not happen often. To shorten the claws, use a pair of fairly sharp scissors, and just remove the tip, taking great care to avoid the quick. If the claws grow quickly, it may be necessary to shorten these each week.

Another typical dogs head study—but of different "type". Photo: Diane Pearce

Feeding the Puppies
For the first 10 to 14 days of their lives the puppies are deaf and their eyes are not open. Gradually little splits will be seen between the eyelids, and eventually the eyes will become completely open. After this stage, they will start to get up on to their feet, and begin to be more active, and will commence to explore the whelping box. Soon after this happens, the puppies can be taught to lap should this be necessary.

At about three weeks of age, they will require some additional food, and should be well able to lap. Start by giving the puppies a supplementary feed of milk, which must be full cream. The best type of product is one of those specially marketed for puppy rearing, but a dried baby milk powder is also very good. Two supplementary feeds should be given daily at first, and by the time the puppies are about 3½ weeks old a baby cereal, such as Farlene, should be added to the milk.

At 3½–4 weeks of age the puppies should be given meat, which should be minced up very fine if fresh meat is being given. It is equally good to feed a tinned meat, providing this has all the lumps finely chopped up.

At 4 weeks of age the puppies should be having three meals a day. A litter of 8 puppies should be having approximately the following quantities:

To be divided amongst 8 puppies.
1. 1½ pts (·85 litre) milk with Farlene and 2 Weetabix
2. 2 oz (57 gms) meat per puppy with 2 Weetabix
3. 1½ pts (·85 litre) milk with Farlene and 2 Weetabix

When the puppies reach this age they will wish to enlarge their horizons as they are now very steady on their feet, and starting tentative games with each other. The front of the whelping box should now be taken out, so that they can run around the kennel, the floor of which should be covered with sawdust. By this time the bitch will start to get bored with her puppies, and will want increasingly longer periods away from them, though she will wish to return to them periodically to feed them, and should be shut in with them at nights.

When the puppies reach 5 weeks, their dam's milk supply will be diminishing, and they will require an additional meal each day, and the meals should now consist of:

To be divided amongst 8 puppies.
1. 2 pts (1·1 litres) milk with Farlene and 4 Weetabix
2. 2 pts (1·1 litres) milk with Farlene and 4 Weetabix
3. 4 oz (113 gms) meat per puppy and 4 Weetabix plus Vitamins and Calcium
4. 2 pts (1·1 litres) milk with Farlene and Weetabix

At 6 weeks old a fine wholemeal biscuit meal can be introduced gradually, but care must be taken not to make the change too quickly, as this can cause tummy upsets. As the biscuit is increased, so the quantities of Farlene and Weetabix can be decreased. If desired, a second meat meal can be substituted for one of the milk meals, and if this is done the feeds will be as given below:

To be divided amongst 8 puppies.
1. 3 pts (1·7 litres) milk with cereal (Weetabix or Biscuit Meal)
2. 3 oz (85 gms) meat per puppy with cereal
3. 3 oz (85 gms) meat per puppy with cereal
4. 3 pts (1·7 litres) milk with Farlene

Am. and Eng. Ch. Figaro of Yeo, a prolific winner.

The quantities should be increased over the next two weeks, until, at 8 weeks old the puppies are having:

To be divided amongst 8 puppies.
1. 4 pts (2·2 litres) milk with biscuit meal
2. 4 oz (113 gms) meat per puppy with biscuit
3. 4 oz (113 gms) meat per puppy with biscuit
4. 4 pts (2·2 litres) milk with Farlene

Throughout this period, and until adulthood, the puppies must be given their additional Calcium and Vitamins, unless tinned meat, with these already added, is being given.

Worming the Puppies

Even though the bitch has been properly wormed when first in whelp, her puppies will still be born with round worms, and these can cause much digestive trouble if not dealt with as soon as reasonably possible. This is at about 3–4 weeks old, and at this time the puppies should be given a worming dose which must be done strictly following the instructions given, to include exact body weight of each puppy being ascertained. You are advised to get tablets from your vet for this purpose, but there are many proprietary preparations on the market which are specifically made for puppies, and any of these which contain Piperazine Citrate are alright. The worming should be repeated at 2-weekly intervals until the puppy goes to its new home, and the new owners should be advised to continue with this process of worming the puppy, until it is three months old.

Hardening the Puppies off
This term means gradually getting the puppies used to less heat, and allowing them to familiarise themselves to the outside world. At about four weeks old they should be living without any additional heat, though they may require their lamp on in cold weather, and at 5–6 weeks, providing the weather is suitable, they can be allowed out for short periods, and then returned to their kennel. If left out it this age they often curl up in a heap, in a corner, on the concrete, and this is not good for them.

Soon after 6 weeks they can be left to their own devices if the weather is warm and sunny. Never leave the puppies out if the weather is wet, for they will soon become wet and miserable, and will be subjected to the danger of catching a chill.

Advertising the Puppies
Advertisements should be sent in to the papers several weeks before the puppies are ready to leave, and do not forget that the papers may take two weeks or more before they insert your advertisement. The best papers in which to advertise the litter are the local ones, and the two dog papers, *Dog World* and *Our Dogs*. Some of the national papers are quite good, but the cost per insertion is high.

Your prospective purchasers will wish to come and choose their puppy when it is at its prettiest – about 5–6 weeks old – though they will not be able to take it home until it is 8 weeks. If, however, the puppy is a future show prospect then the earliest it should be chosen is 8 weeks, as puppies change so much up to this age, and the best puppy at 6 weeks can be quite inferior to others at 8 weeks.

Instructions and Documentation for the New Owner
The new owner should be given a list of all the "do's and don't's" entailed in having a new puppy. Instructions on feeding, inoculating, worming and house-training should be given,

otherwise your telephone will never stop ringing with worried puppy owner's questions.

The full pedigree should be given when the puppy is collected, and the purchasers told that the Kennel Club papers will be sent as soon as possible – these should have been applied for soon after the puppies' birth.

Ch. Camrose Nicolas of Westley (whelped 1957), winner of 20 C.C.s.

Chapter 9

Showing your Golden Retriever

Conditioning

If the dog is to be shown, he must be in the correct condition and carrying the right amount of flesh. He should be nicely covered over the ribs and loins, but not excessively so, and should have no tendency to "roll" when moving. When looked at from above, if correctly conditioned, he should have nicely rounded ribs and should not be straight from the shoulder to the hindquarters, for the loins should go in slightly behind the ribs.

It is an easy matter to fatten the dog up a little should this be necessary, and should not take too long, but it is no easy matter to slim down an overweight Golden. To do so, all biscuits or bread must be cut out and the daily diet should consist of only 8 oz (227 gms) of meat for a bitch and 12 oz (340 gms) of meat for a dog. Additional exercise must also be given, and this is a good idea for any dog, as it tones up and develops the muscles.

Trimming

To put a Golden in the showring looking immaculate needs far more work than the average novice owner imagines, for some dogs look very unkempt without any trimming, and with their coats unbathed. To make a really professional job of the trimming you will require thinning scissors, ordinary sharp scissors and a metal comb. A Duplex trimming knife is also an asset, but not essential.

The easiest way to start trimming is at the front of the dog and work back, so start with the ears first, then do the neck and shoulders, then front feet. Next attend to the hocks and back feet, and, lastly, the tail.

Ears

Use the thinning scissors to take out all the long hairs above, and at the sides of the ears. Always use the thinning scissors in an upward direction, following the line of the hairs' growth, and

The breed's all-time top winner with 41 C.C.s—Ch. Camrose Cabus Christopher—is also the breed's top sire. Cabus has two Best In Shows to his credit as well as eight Gundog Groups. Photo: Diane Pearce

comb the loose hair out frequently – preferably after two or three cuts. When the outer-side of the ear is completed do the under-side, and thin all the long hairs at the base of the ear cavity.

Neck
Starting at the breast bone, and still using the thinning scissors, thin the front of the neck, again in an upward direction, until all the surplus hair has been removed. The neck should give a smooth appearance and have no long hairs detracting from the neatness of the dog. The neck should be thinned out both at the front and at the sides, right up under the ears.

Shoulders
These, if trimmed well, can enhance the look tremendously, and can display the dog's length of neck so much better. Often a dog with a reasonably long neck can look "stuffy", or short, thick necked, if not trimmed properly.

Good friends! Photo: Diane Pearce

All the long hair covering the shoulders should be thinned out, again using the thinning scissors, until there is a smooth finish, and all unnecessary hair has been removed. The hair must be removed in an upward direction, following the line of the hairs' growth.

Care must be taken when first attempting to thin shoulders, for, if not correctly done, this can completely ruin the look of the dog. It is a good idea to trim the dog a long time before you intend to show him, so that the hair has time to grow again before the show date should you spoil his looks.

Front Feet

These should be tidied up with ordinary scissors, and should have the outline of the foot trimmed back as near to the top of the pads as possible, in order to make the foot look cat-like and rounded. Some Goldens grow quite a lot of hair between their pads, both between the toes and on the under-sides. This should be trimmed off, the hair between the toes being pulled forward, and a better finish is given if the hair is cut in a downward direction.

Hocks
Many Goldens grow a considerable amount of hair on the back of their hocks, and this is tidied up with the scissors, and any surplus long hair covering the top of the hocks from the "trousers" should be taken out with the thinning scissors.

Hindleg Feathering (or Trousers)
Some Goldens grow excessive hindleg feathering, and if this is too thick and long, it can give an unbalanced look. This can be thinned out and shortened with the thinning scissors. Use an upward cut for thinning, but cut across if they need shortening.

Back Feet
These should be trimmed exactly as for the front feet, leaving a neat tidy look. Feet that are well trimmed can appear so much

Dutch F.T.Ch. and Ch. Andy van Sparrenrode, winning from Golden Chap Beijeren. Photo: Wim v Vugh

tighter and smaller than beforehand, and if the feet are not of the correct shape, at least they will be improved by careful trimming.

Tail

The long feathering on the underside of the tail should be shortened, and the hair taken back to about $\frac{1}{2}$ inch (1·2 cm) from the tip. There can be no hard and fast rule as to the exact length of the feathering to be left on the tail, as this so much depends on the size of the dog. A large dog would not look balanced if the hair is too short on the tail, nor would a small dog look balanced with too much hair left on.

To see the shape, and approximate length desirable, it is a good idea to study the photographs of some of the Champions of the day, such as those appearing in this book, and try to copy these. The tail can be trimmed with scissors or thinning scissors, and if too bushy should be thinned out, in an upward direction.

Bathing and Drying

Full details of bathing the dog have been given in Chapter 5, so it will only be necessary to deal with the drying process, which must be very carefully done for a show dog, especially if your dog's coat is wavy.

After bathing, which you are recommended to do the day before the show, your dog should be rough dryed, and then the coat combed into position. A warm, sunny day helps the drying process very much, for whilst the coat is drying on the top, the dog can be made to stand with his back in the sun, and the coat constantly combed into place, until nearly dry. This stops pieces of hair drying in the wrong position. However, warm, sunny days are not often to be had in this country, so it is usually necessary to resort to other methods.

A hair dryer is excellent, but the hair must constantly be combed into place. The other ideal drying procedure is to sit the dog near an electric fire, and set the hair by combing whilst drying. All these varying ways of drying the dog take time, but do pay dividends, particularly on a wavy-coated dog. However, if time is precious, and an easier method is required, then the dog may be dried by rugging it up. This is when a towel or rug is tied around the dog to keep the hair in place, and this must be left in position until the dog is completely dry. It certainly is a time-saving method, but one doubts if the dog appreciates being dressed up!

If the dog's coat is straight, it is not nearly such a problem to dry, for as long as it is periodically combed into place, it should present no difficulties.

Am. Ch. Beaumaris Dalesman C.D., bred by Anne Bissette and owned by Arlene Recktenwald, seen winning Best of Breed in 1976.

When dry, the coat must be well brushed with a wire hound glove as this imparts a wonderful sheen to the coat, and then finished off with a metal comb.

Training your Dog for the Showring

Before you enter your dog for a show, he must be trained to do what is required of him. He must be taught to trot without pulling on the leash, to stand still and in correct show stance whilst the judge examines him, and this includes looking at the teeth. The easiest way to learn how to show the dog is to attend ringcraft classes, which are held by most Dog Show Societies. These help to teach both you and the dog the correct method of showing.

When a dog is shown at a benched show he will have to be chained up to his bench all day, and a dog not used to being tied up will resent this very much. It is useful to get the dog accustomed to this by tying him up whilst at home for short periods, so that this will not be a new and frightening experience to him.

Entering your Dog for a Show

In order to compete in a show the dog must first be registered with the Kennel Club in the Active Register, in the owner's name.

Advertisements for the various shows are given each week in Dog World and Our Dogs, and they announce the date for entries closing. You will require a schedule of the show which can be obtained from the Secretary, and you must then complete all the dog's details on the entry form – name, sex, date of birth, breeder's name, name of sire and dam, and numbers of the classes in which he is to be entered. This must then be sent to the secretary of the show society, together with the necessary entry fees, by the date mentioned in the schedule. This is usually about a month prior to the show.

Types of Shows

Exemption shows. These shows are exempt from Kennel Club Licence, and are generally run in conjunction with local fetes on behalf of charities. To enter at these the dog need not be Kennel Club registered, and any wins there do not count when entering for a Kennel Club Licenced show.

Irish and Eng. Ch. Bryanstown Gale Warning. Photo: Thomas Fall

Sanction shows. These are small shows, usually of about 20 classes, which are confined to members, and restrict the entry to dogs which have not won their way out of Post-Graduate classes. Those which have won five or more first prizes in Post-Graduate or higher classes are not allowed to enter. These shows, of course, exclude Challenge Certificate winners, and usually consist of Any Variety Classes i.e. those catering for all breeds. Wins here do not count when entering for Open or Championship shows.

Limited shows. These are also restricted to members and exclude all Challenge Certificate winners. Wins at these shows do not count when entering for Open or Championship Shows. They usually have some classes catering for specific breeds, but most of the classes are for Any Varieties.

Open shows. These shows are open to all exhibitors and dogs, and usually have three or four classes for the most popular breeds in the area, but also have a number of Any Variety Classes. Wins at these shows count when entering in future Open or Championship Shows, and a first at an Open Show adds one point for a dog under 18 months old trying for a Junior Warrant.

Championship shows. These shows are open to all exhibitors and dogs, and have Kennel Club Challenge Certificates on offer for most of the breeds scheduled, and these awards are the most cherished of all in the showring. There is, however, one show at which entries are restricted to dogs which have qualified by winning at another Championship Show, and this is the one run by the Kennel Club, namely Crufts. There are many Championship Shows held throughout the British Isles (except for Eire, which does not come under our Kennel Club's jurisdiction) and seasoned exhibitors will probably attend about 25 of these shows a year. A first-prize win at a Championship Show counts three points towards a Junior Warrant.

Championship Shows usually schedule a number of classes for each breed, such as Puppy, Junior, Maiden, Novice, Under-graduate, Graduate, Post-Graduate, Limit and Open, and most of these will be divided according to the sex of the exhibit. Naturally, the more popular breeds will have more of these classes given to them than the less popular. The Puppy and Junior classes are restricted by age limits, but all other classes restrict the entries according to the amount of winning the dog has achieved.

Kennel Club Challenge Certificates. These are awarded to the best of each sex at Championship Shows, providing the judge is of the opinion that the dog is of such outstanding merit as to be worthy of the title of Champion.

"Setting up" a puppy to assess its show potential. Photo: Diane Pearce

Kennel Club Titles

Show Champion. This title is awarded to a gundog which has won three Challenge Certificates under three different judges.

Champion. To become a Champion a gundog must win three Challenge Certificates under three different judges and also be awarded a Qualifying Certificate (see later in the Chapter).

Field Trial Champion. A gundog is awarded this title when it has won either two Open Any Variety Retriever Stakes, or one Open Any Variety Stake and one All-Aged Stake run for its own breed, or wins the Retriever Championship.

Dual Champion. Dual Champion is the highest title which can be obtained by a gundog and is a dog which has become both a Field Trial Champion and a Champion at shows. There have, in this breed, only been three such title-holders in the whole of the post-war period.

Obedience Champion. A dog must win three Obedience Challenge Certificates under three different judges in order to qualify for this title, or win the Obedience Certificate at Crufts, and entry into this competition at Crufts is restricted to dogs which have won Obedience Certificates during the previous year.

Junior Warrant. This is awarded to a dog which has won 25 points in all at Open or Championship shows before he reaches the age of 18 months. A first prize at an Open Show counts 1 point. A first prize at a Championship Show counts 3 points.

Qualifying Certificate. To be given the title of Champion all gundogs must be awarded a Qualifying Certificate at a recognised Field Trial, or at a meeting run specifically for this purpose by a specialist breed club, and there must be two Kennel Club List A judges officiating.

The requirements for a Qualifying Certificate are that the dog shall be tested in the line and prove that it is not gunshy, will hunt and retrieve tenderly to hand.

Equipment to Take to the Show

The exhibitor needs quite an amount of equipment with him when going to a show, so it is advisable to get things ready the night before the show. A bag of some description will be needed to take all the dog's belongings, and these must include a hound glove, comb, benching chain, a show leash (I like a nylon slipleash which is not too wide), cleansing powder, coat grooming sprays, water bowl, water container, food, towels, rug for the bench and safety pin or similar for the ring card number.

Chapter 10

Training to the Gun and Field Trials

The early, basic obedience training of walking to heel, sitting, staying and recall have all been discussed earlier, so that by this time you should have a dog which is ready to start the actual work of a retriever.

Early Exercises

You will require a whistle for the next stages of the training, for the dog should be taught to sit when you blow one long blast, at the same time holding your hand up in front of him. For the recall he should be taught to come when you blow several short blasts.

From his early days he should have been encouraged to carry things, and bring them to you, so that no bad habits have been formed. It is fatal with a dog required for gun-work to have one to train which has been discouraged from picking things up, and has been scolded for so doing.

The actual serious training should not start until the dog is about 8 months old, when he should be made to sit, whilst you throw a dummy, this can be made out of a stuffed sock or be one of the canvas type. He should be allowed to see the fall of the dummy, and after a minute or two, be allowed to go and pick it up on the command "Get out" accompanied by a forward wave of your arm. If he should show any reluctance to come back to you when he has picked it up, encourage him by calling his name, and start running away from him, or adopt a crouching position. These methods frequently make the dog come straight to you. Only one or two retrieves should be given at a time, and the training session must always finish on a good note, with the dog having completed his exercise correctly.

It is advisable to give short heel, sit and stay lessons at each training session, as well as making him sit, walking away from him, and whistling him up to you. Use the whistle as much as possible at this stage in the training, for the use of this for the sit and recall are the most essential basics for a well-trained dog, and for one which is to be trialled, for they are the beginnings of "distance control". When the dog can be left sitting at a good distance away from you, then he can be recalled part of the way, and if well-drilled in the sit exercise, he should sit when you blow the whistle and raise your arm in front of you. Should he complete this exercise satisfactorily he can then be recalled to you and given much praise.

Gun-fire

The dog should first be introduced to gun-fire with the aid of a starting pistol. This does not make too loud a noise but gets the dog used to associating the gun being fired with the fact that something interesting is happening. Stand a short distance away from the dog, who should be in a sitting position, then throw a dummy and fire the starting pistol. The dog's attention is thus on the thrown dummy rather than on the loud bang. If the dog does not appear startled, then the pistol can be fired closer to him.

Miss Lumsden handling in a Field Trial. Photo: Roland Clarke

When he has become quite accustomed to this starting pistol then real gun-fire can be introduced – but stand a good distance away from the dog for the first time or two that the gun is being fired. Then proceed as before.

Retrieving from Cover
To encourage the dog to hunt and use his nose, when he is proficient at retrieving dummies visible to him, start throwing them into light cover. Tell him to "Get out" and wave your arm as directed earlier, and when he starts searching in the cover encourage him by saying "Hie lost". He will soon associate these words with the fact that he is searching in the correct place, and should soon locate the dummy. Repeat this on several days using the same piece or pieces of cover, so that he associates these places as being somewhere in which to find dummies. The next stage in the "unseen dummy" exercise is to hide a dummy in the cover before you take him out of the kennel, then take him quite near to the hidden dummy, and send him in that direction, by saying "Get out" and waving your arm. Having had success in

The best way for a Golden to travel—especially if there is mud around—is in an estate car, the straw will help clean him. Photo: Diane Pearce

Ch. Synspur Lunic. Photo: Thomas Fall

this place on previous occasions he will be sure to hunt there again. As he becomes proficient in this, you can then vary the cover in which you hide the dummy, and he should have learnt that hunting can bring forth rewards. Gradually lengthen the distance you take him away from the cover before sending him out. This hunting for something unseen is one of the very important parts of a gundog's training.

Retrieving from Water
Most Goldens take very easily to water, and in fact are difficult to keep out of it. They should be introduced to it at about six months of age, at a place with easy access. If an older dog is taken with the puppy this will encourage the younger one to go in, as he will wish to follow his older companion, and soon he will be swimming around too.

As he gets used to the water, so he can be given a dummy to retrieve from it, then later, he should be taken to a fairly narrow

95

(Above and opposite) A Golden seen retrieving Teal.

stream, and the dummy should be thrown on to the opposite side in the open. When he has successfully completed this exercise several times, he can then have the dummy thrown across the water and into cover on the opposite bank when he will have to hunt for the dummy before being able to retrieve it.

Steadiness

This is a most important thing to achieve in a gundog, for a dog which "runs in" to gun-fire, or chases game is most objectionable – and would not be tolerated in Field Trials.

To instil steadiness into the dog it is essential that implicit obedience is taught in the early stages, and the dog must never be allowed to "break" or "run in" when a dummy is thrown. He must always sit and wait until commanded to retrieve. Accustom him to seeing several dummies thrown around him when he is sitting, and also whilst he is retrieving, and check immediately any sign of unsteadiness.

Direction Training

This is a must for a working dog, for so much time can be wasted and wounded birds lost, if a dog is hunting in the wrong place.

Sit the dog and walk away from him, having two dummies with you. Turn to face him, and instil into him the fact that he must stay, then throw one dummy to your left and the other to your

96

right. Wave your arm in the direction of the first dummy thrown and command him to "Get out". The chances are that he will start out in the direction of the last one thrown. As soon as he moves in the wrong direction, blow your whistle and make him sit again, then re-direct him in the correct direction. Repeat the process until success has been achieved. When he has successfully retrieved the first dummy, then send him for the other.

Gradually increase the distance you walk away from the dog before throwing the dummies, and as you reach a high standard, you should be able to direct him to several dummies thrown in slightly different directions.

When this training is perfected you should then be able to send the dog out, stop him on the whistle, and re-direct him to whichever dummy you wish retrieved, gradually increasing the length of the retrieves.

Jumping

The dog should not be taught to jump until his muscles are well-developed, and he is about a year old. He should then be taken into a narrow enclosed pathway, in which have been constructed several low jumps. Throw the dummy along this pathway and give the command "Over". If the dog is to retrieve the dummy he must first negotiate the jumps, and, by this time his instinct to retrieve should be so strongly implanted that he will do so. Gradually increase the height of the jumps, and as he learns the command "Over" you can take him out of the pathway, and try him over an ordinary jump, such as a low fence, or a gate. Later he should be able to negotiate anything as high as a five-barred gate – but do avoid any fences with barbed wire on top.

Introducing to Game

This should never be done until the dog has been taught implicit obedience, and has achieved a good standard of retrieving of dummies. Introducing him to game too early in life can cause him to become unsteady later. The best type of dead game to start him with is a small hen pheasant, which is quite easy to carry. Allow him to smell the pheasant, which should be reasonably freshly shot, and walk with him to heel, then sit him and throw the bird. When sent for it he will usually pick it up fairly readily and should be praised and encouraged to bring it back to you. Should he be hesitant about picking it, it is a good idea to let him hold it in his mouth and carry it whilst walking to heel.

If, however, the dog is still reluctant to pick up the pheasant, placing it in a nylon stocking sometimes helps. Another method to encourage the dog to pick feather is to remove the wings from a pheasant and tie these round his dummy. I had one bitch, who eventually became a super "picking up" dog, who refused all my efforts to make her to retrieve feather, until I let her pick a dummy with pheasant wings around it, then transferred these same wings to the body of a hen pheasant. Having retrieved her usual wings attached to a bird, she then progressed by carrying the bird without them! After that she never looked back.

Having successfully taught your Golden to retrieve cold game, it must be left to the shooting day to introduce him to freshly shot game, but most dogs will readily accept this once they are used to cold game.

Do not let him pick a wounded bird, or one which is running, too early in his shoting days, as this can cause hard-mouth, or make the dog unsteady. Only allow him to retrieve dead game for the first part of the shooting season.

Training Classes

These are held in various parts of the country, and are particularly useful for the novice trainer who aspires to run his dog in either Working Tests or Field Trials. Before attending these classes it is advisable that the dog's basic obedience and retrieving work is fairly proficient, so that he will be ready to take on the usual more advanced training to the gun.

Working Tests

These are organised by the various clubs holding the training classes, and are not Kennel Club recognised events. They consist of various exercises to show the dog's proficiency in heel-work, his steadiness to gun-fire and falling dummies, his ability to retrieve seen and unseen dummies, his direction control and to test his prowess in and across water. These tests are always carried out on dummies.

Cold Game Tests

As the name implies, these are tests, similar to those used in Working Tests, but with the use of cold game instead of dummies.

Field Trials

These events have the recognition of the Kennel Club and dogs competing in these have their wins recorded in the Kennel Club Stud Book. There are various types of trials, according to either the age of the dog or to its amount of winning. Trials are run actually on a shooting day, with game being retrieved as it is shot. Some trials consist of walking up, and others have part walking up and part drives.

There are either three or four judges, more usually three, in which case each dog is tested in the line under two judges, generally being given two retrieves each time. Then the judges

An excellent group study showing various coat colours. Photo: Diane Pearce

confer and the best dogs are brought back for further testing. When there are four judges, they work in pairs, each pair having two dogs in line at a time.

The varying categories of trials are those for Puppies (dogs under two years old), Non-Winners and Open and All-Aged Stakes. Some are run by breed societies for their own breed, whilst others are organised by Field Trial Societies, and cater for all breeds of Retrievers. Wins in Any Variety Open Stakes qualify the dog to enter into the Retriever Championship, as do All-Aged Stakes for Goldens. The qualifications required to enable a dog to run in the Retriever Championship are rather complicated, but are based on the particular trial and the awards won.

The Retriever Championship is run annually, and naturally with its stiff qualifications, has only the best of the Retrievers for that year running. Only two Goldens have won this trial during the post-war period.

Ch. Teecon Ambassador. Photo: Diane Pearce

Appendix 1

BIBLIOGRAPHY

Charlesworth, Mrs. W. M.
  1947 *The Golden Retriever*, Fletcher & Son Ltd., Norwich.
Croxton-Smith, A.
  1950 *Dogs Since 1900*, Andrew Dakers.
Elliott, Rachael Page
  1973 *Dog Steps: Illustrated Gait At A Glance*, Howell Book House Inc., New York.
Harmer, Hilary
  1968 *Dogs and How to Breed Them*, John Gifford.
Moxon, P. R. A.
  1952 *Gundogs: Training & Field Trials*, Popular Dogs Pub. Co., London.
  1977 *Training The Rough Shooters Dog*, Popular Dogs Pub. Co., London.
Sharp R.
  1924 *Gun Training For Amateurs*, Country Life, London.
Smythe, R. H.
  1962 *The Anatomy Of Dog Breeding*, Popular Dogs Pub. Co., London.
Stonex, Elma
  1953 *The Golden Retriever Handbook*, Nicholson & Watson, Redhill.
Tudor, Joan
  1966 *The Golden Retriever*, Popular Dogs Pub. Co., London.
White, Kay
  1978 *Dogs: Their Mating, Whelping and Weaning*, K & R Books Ltd., Horncastle.

Appendix 2

SPECIALIST BREED CLUBS

GOLDEN RETRIEVER CLUB
  Hon Sec. Mrs. T. Theed, Squirrels Brook, Salters Green,
  Mayfield, Sussex.
NORTHERN GOLDEN RETRIEVER ASSOCIATION
  Hon. Sec. Mrs. M. Dawson, The Poplars,
  Donington Northorpe, Spalding, Lincs.
GOLDEN RETRIEVER CLUB OF WALES
  Hon. Sec. Mrs. M. Hunton-Girling, Sarelle, Ponthir,
  Newport, Gwent.
GOLDEN RETRIEVER CLUB OF SCOTLAND
  Hon. Sec. Mrs. M. Smart, 5 Strathearn Tce., Perth, Scotland.
ULSTER GOLDEN RETRIEVER CLUB.
  Hon. Sec. Mr. W. H. Hosford, 4 Gortin Ave., Comber,
  Co. Down, N. Ireland.
SOUTH WESTERN GOLDEN RETRIEVER CLUB
  Hon. Sec. Mr. R. Coward, Green Acres, Ibsley Drive,
  Fordingbridge, Nr. Ringwood, Hants.
MIDLAND GOLDEN RETRIEVER CLUB
  Hon. Sec. Mr. R. Taylor, The Red House, Belle Vue Lane,
  Blidworth, Notts.
SOUTHERN GOLDEN RETRIEVER SOCIETY
  Hon. Sec. Mrs. M. Pounds, Folly Farm, Staplehurst, Kent.
EASTERN COUNTIES GOLDEN RETRIEVER CLUB
  Hon. Sec. Mr. D. T. Willey, 152 Winstree Rd., Stanway,
  Colchester, Essex.
GOLDEN RETRIEVER CLUB OF NORTHUMBRIA
  Hon. Sec. Mrs. J. Hay, 12 Hedley Rd., Seaton Delaval,
  Whitley Bay, Tyne and Wear.
*BERKSHIRE DOWNS AND CHILTERNS GOLDEN RETRIEVER
CLUB*
  Hon. Sec. Mrs. E. Henbest, Bank Green Cottage, Bellington,
  Chesham, Bucks.

Index

(*Italic figures denote illustration*)

Ailments   42
Alresford Advertiser, Ch.   20
Atkinson, Mrs. J.   21, 22
Aurora   17

Balcombe Boy, Dual Ch.   16
Balcombe Bunty   17
Baldwin, Mr.   21
Balvaig   17
Barron, Mrs.   22
Bathing   39, 42, 86
Belle   13
Binks of Kentford   17
Birkin, Mrs. V.   22
Borrow, Mrs. E.   22
Breeding
    In-breeding   61
    Line-breeding   60
    Out-crossing   61
Brood bitch   58

Cabus Boltby Combine, Int.
    Ch.   22
Cabus Cadet, Int. Ch.   22
Camrose Cabus Christopher,
    Ch.   20, 22, *83*
Camrose Evenpatrol, Int. Ch.   *56*
Camrose Fantango, Ch.   22
Camrose Nicolas of Westley,
    Ch.   *18*, 20, 22, *81*
Camrose Tallyrand of Anbria,
    Ch.   20, 22
Carnegie, The Hon. D.   16, 18
Charlesworth, Mrs. W. M.   15,
    18, 19
Cindy Fan It Fokheehoal, Int.
    Ch.   *10*

Cornelius, Ch.   17
Cottingham, Mrs.   17
Cubbington Diver, Ch.   17
Culham Brass   16
Culham Copper   16

Davern Figaro, Ch.   *9*
David of Westley, Int. Dual
    Ch.   20
Davie of Yelme, Ch.   17, *19*
Dew claws   73
Diet
    Adult   82
    Puppy to 8 weeks   30
    Puppy after 8 weeks   31
Diver of Woolley   17
Dorcas Bruin   22
Dorcas Glorious of Slat, Ch.   22
Dorcas Leola   22
Dorcas Timberscombe Topper   22

Eccles, Mr. and Mrs.   16, 18
Exercise   37
External parasites   42

Feeding   (*see under Diet*)
Field Trials   92, 99

Gilder   17
Gill, Miss J.   20, 22
Glory of Fyning   16
Golden Camrose Tess   22
Grigg, The Hon. Mrs.   16
Grooming   32, 39
Guide Dogs   10

Harrison, Mrs. (Boltby)   20, 22

Heydown Grip, Ch.   17
Hickmott, Mr. W.   20
Holway Gaiety, F.T. Ch.   22
Holway Teal of Westley, F.T.
   Ch.   21
Holway Zest, F.T. Ch.   21, 22

Iles, Wing-Com. and Mrs.   22
Inoculations   40

Jenner, Mr. H.   16, 17
Jessamy, Mr.   20

Kennel Club
   Field Trials   92, 99
   Shows   88
   Standard   45
   Titles and awards   89, 90
Kirk, Mr. R. L.   17

le Poer Trench, Col.   16
Lord Tweedmouth   13
Lowe, Mr. and Mrs.   22
Lumsden, Mrs. J.   21

Macdonald, Mr. D.   16
Matings   61
Mazurka of Wynford, F.T. Ch.   21
Medhurst, Mrs. G.   22
Michael of Moreton, Ch.   *17*
Minter, Mrs. E.   22
Moriarty, Mrs.   20, 22
Mountain Rescue   11

Nairn, Mrs. and Miss S.   18
Noranby Destiny, Dual Ch.   16,
   20
Nous   13

Palgrave Holway Folly, F.T.
   Ch.   22
Parsons, Mrs. I.   18
Philpott, Mrs. D.   22
Pilkington, Mrs. L.   20
Pippa of Westley, Ch.   *32*
Puppies
   Care after 8 weeks   80
   Care to 8 weeks   77
   Choosing   23, 26

Rearing   30

Registration   29
Ringmaster of Yeo   22
Robertson, Mrs. P.   21, 22
Rory of Bentley   17
Rossbourne Timothy, Sh. Ch.   *11*

Sawtell, Mrs. L.   22
Showing
   Entering   88
   Preparation for   86, 91
   Training for   87
   Trimming for   82
Shows, types of   88
Siggers, Mr. Bill   49
Simon of Westley, Ch.   20
Smythe, R. H.   49
Stagden Cross Pamela   16
Stolford Happy Lad, Ch.   21, *48*
Stonex, Mrs. E.   14, 16, 22
Stubblesdown Golden Lass, Dual
   Ch.   20, 22
Stud Dog   59

Temperature   72
Timson, Mrs. M.   22
Tiranti, Mr. and Mrs.   22
Training
   Car   33
   Gun   92
   House   33
   Leash   35
   Obedience   33
Treunair Cala, F.T. Ch.   21
Tudor, Mrs. J.   22
Tweed-Water Spaniel   13

Venables Kirk, Mr. and Mrs.   18

Wentworth Smith, Mr.   17
Whelping   68
Whelping Box   67
Whelping Quarters   66
Wilcock, Miss R.   22
Winston, Mrs. S.   (*see Nairn,
   Miss S.*)
Worming   29, 41, 79

DATE   wieght
4/5/80   12lb

HARVEY - Golden Retriever dog.